OVER

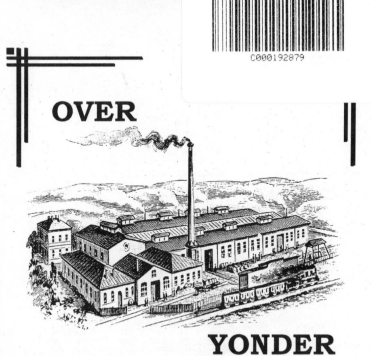

YONDER

Last of the
Shoddy Town Tales

by

Fred Butler

illustrated by Graham Kaye

FAB Publications

First published in 2003

by

FAB Publications

Eastfield House

Flash Lane

Mirfield

West Yorkshire

WF14 0PU

Tel/Fax 01924 492249

© 2003 Fred Butler

ISBN 0-9540683-2-7

Illustrations by Graham Kaye

Brighouse   West Yorkshire   01484 712752

Printed in Great Britain by

Priory Press

Dedicated

to

Mum and Dad

who had the foresight to

bring me to the Shoddy Towns

to grow up

CONTENTS

***

OVER YONDER

IN HECKMONDWIKE

I first learned the classroom value of a good tale very early on in my teaching career - at Batley Boys' High School in 1966, to be precise. Confronted by thirty or so reluctant Shoddy Town lads, it was my educational task to get them to write essays, contrary to their collective wishes. So somehow, I'd got to inspire them to put pen to paper. How on earth was I going to do it?

During my previous three years' training at Goldsmiths' College, none of my lecturers/tutors had actually come up with the ideal solution to this most pressing of educational problems. It was very much left to me to fend for myself. Wracking my brains to devise some method to promote creative writing amongst my pupils, I arrived at a workable solution quite by accident one dull autumn morning. I was desperately trying to capture the interest of my third year class of lads, before setting them the task of writing a "composition" when, out of the blue, plucked somewhere from the philosophical ether above my head, I invented a life-long pal from Heckmondwike called Wilberforce who got himself into all sorts of adventurous scrapes.

I noticed that, at the mention of "my mate Wilberforce from over yonder in Heckmondwike", the lads in front of me showed a fairly keen interest, and they began to pay attention.

Thinking that I was onto an educational ploy of some importance, I proceeded to lie my head off about Wilberforce's adventures and all the exciting scrapes he got himself into. At the most intriguing, cliff-hanging moment in my tale, I would stop and ask the lads to complete the story for themselves, in writing, in their own words.

To my astonishment, they set to with an enthusiasm hitherto unwitnessed, and from that point on, throughout my teaching career, I used the technique in all sorts of varying educational situations. Of course, good teachers had been using the self-same ploy for generations, so it was nothing new. But for Yours Truly, at that long-gone moment in October, 1966, I thought I had made an educational breakthrough of astounding proportions.

The habit stuck and the teaching content of my lessons throughout the following thirty years often took second place to an egocentric tale-telling session. At my very mention of the words "Did I ever tell you about the time when I ...", my class would down pens and lean back in their seats. A smile of contentment would light up many of the adolescent faces in front of me as they perceived the next ten minutes to be a "sit-back-and-relax" session.

As an educational technique, I'm not so sure that it was entirely successful. Working on the premise that pupils who are enjoying their time in my classroom might also learn their scholastic work more effectively, I doggedly stuck to my tale-telling guns for the next thirty years, right up until my retirement in 1996. I enjoyed *every* minute of *every* tale told in *every* lesson - so much so that I put pen to paper and told them all again in "Up the Snicket" and "Down the Ginnel".

But what has amazed me over the past forty years [and continues to do so], is that all my tales have their roots in the uncomplicated events of a fairly ordinary life amongst the people of the Heavy Woollen District. From the moment I stepped down onto Bradford Road from the platform of the Number 20 Yorkshire Woollen District Transport Omnibus [Leeds-Mirfield via Batley] one spring morning in 1957, it has always been the good people of Dewsbury, Batley and the Spen Valley who have been the inspiration for all my stories. Their down-to-earth sense of humour and their determination to have a "reight good laugh" have provided me with many a comic moment to record for posterity. My thanks to you all.

So now, I offer this final collection of tales as the result of a wonderful life earning, learning and laughing alongside genuine Shoddy Town folk. A "comer-in" of some forty-five years standing, I hope that I have now finally earned some credibility as a genuine Shoddy Town lad.

* * *

Fred Butler

May 2003

MISCHIEF

NIGHT

Of all the occasions in my Shoddy Town childhood's year, Mischief Night was the one which gave me the most pleasure. I don't mean pleasure in the Happy Birthday/Merry Christmas /Give-Me-My-Presents sense . No, this was more in the form of a Running Up and Down in the Dark/Adrenalin-Charged/Getting-Away-With-It sort of pleasure.

When I look back to those early days of my Heavy Woollen District life, I realise now that Mischief Night was joyful licence to misbehave. For us thirteen year-olds, it represented permission from the adult world to commit as many "naughties" in the space of two or three hours' darkness on November 4th as we dared to commit for the rest of the year put together...

On our way home from school on my very first pre-Mischief Night afternoon, rotund, dark-haired Pongo Dixon makes a casual enquiry, down by the Bar House. Historically speaking, it was probably on November 3rd, 1958.

There's a mischievous twinkle in Pongo's eye as he puts the question: "Oh, Freddie! Ar ta comin' mischievin' wi' us tomorn neet, then?"

Pongo lived up our road, near the Yew Tree pub, and he had a reputation at Heckmondwike Grammar School for being a bit of a lad. He was a leading light in our Huddersfield

Road gang, which included Roy Wetherall, Danny Parkin and Sam Johnson.

I'd fallen in with them all, shortly after arriving in Yorkshire, largely as a result of geographical location - we all lived around the area of Liversedge, Roberttown and Norristhorpe. But the strange phenomenon about the gang was that amongst the five of us, we represented four different local grammar schools - Batley, Whitcliffe Mount, Heckmondwike and Kaye's College [Huddersfield]. So the gang and its activities was the bonding activity during our developing adolescence. Together, we learned to smoke Woodbines sitting on the seat outside Mitton's Bar House shop, lit fires in the old, abandoned house off Roberttown Lane, made dams on Lands Beck and attended the Saturday night pictures at The Palace in Heckmondwike.

In truth, I was an outsider - a comer-in from "dahn South", and at the time I'm talking about, I was still carrying out my Gang-stipulated Apprenticeship. It had kicked off, quite successfully, I thought, with my mimicking the Shoddy Town mode of speech as a defence against biting sarcasm.

I'd never, in all my young life to date, heard of "Mischief Night".

To Pongo's current enquiry, I replied in a fair mock-up of Shoddy Town dialect: " 'Ow's ta mean, *mischievin*'? Wot's *mischievin*'?"

Now Pongo was a good lad, so he didn't fall about in fits of sarcastic laughter at my lack of knowledge in matters relating to rudimentary local folk-lore. Instead, he clued me in with admirably succinct detail:"Well, thee an' thi mates guz abaht at neet an' tha gets up ter as much bother as tha can. Everybody knows abaht it, so tha dun't get bollocked ser much if tha gets copped."

To my thirteen year-old way of reckoning, this sounded like an admirable arrangement. Naughty tricks around and about the dark streets and no subsequent adult rollickings? It sounded too good to be true.

But Pongo failed to provide me with any background historical information to explain the folk-lore of "Mischief Night".

For a start, he didn't tell me that the practice of "mischievin'" is generally unknown outside Yorkshire. And secondly, he omitted to inform me that Guy Fawkes was a Yorkshireman by birth who lived at Farnley Hall, near Otley and who, in 1606 was intent on blowing the King of England [and Scotland] to smithereens. But Pongo's biggest omission was forgetting to tell me that Guy and his pals would have been up to their dastardly deeds underneath the Houses of Parliament on the night of November 4th all those years ago.

They'd have been dragging their barrels of High Explosive and their fuses across that cellar floor, ready for tomorrow's incendiary activity, no doubt chuckling away to themselves at the prospect of getting rid of the unwanted monarch. So, in Yorkshire at any rate, the tradition had lasted all those years.

And here was I, some three hundred and fifty years down the time-line, going through my Gang-apprenticeship, copying Mr Fawkes's naughty behaviour and learning about creating modern mayhem on the dark streets of 1958.

"We're all off up to t'Yew Tree at half-six tomorn neet. Then we's'll be 'avin' some fun," enthuses Pongo. He winks knowingly at me outside our house and trundles off on his roly-poly way up Huddersfield Road for a bit of tea and a spot of homework.

As darkness falls on the night of November 4th, 1958, I'm all keyed up and anxious to get on with the action. I've skated through my homework, promising myself that I'll copy most of it from Pearsall's book in the pre-school cloakrooms tomorrow morning. I race downstairs from my bedroom, don suitably dark clothes [for camouflage] and lie to my Mum and Dad about going round to Roy Wetherall's house to borrow a rubber for my English essay. I sidle to the back door and make my naughty way outside.

Roy is already at our gate, hopping up and down in eager anticipation. He, too, is suitably clad for mischieving and together, we amble up to The Yew Tree pub on the corner of Norristhorpe Lane.

Under the street-lamp, the rest of the gang are already there - armed to the teeth.

Danny Parkin has his pockets stuffed full of tuppenny cannons*; Sam "Kipper" Johnson has yards of white washing-line slung round his shoulder, pinched from the top of their cellar-steps; Pongo Dixon has an old envelope full of drawing-pins, filched from a teacher's untidy desk-top; and Roy has a reel of black cotton from his Mum's unguarded sewing-box. Each member of the gang

*tuppenny cannon: a "banger" of immense sonic power -
the most powerful available at Lucas's
shop on Norristhorpe Lane

carries either a torch or a cycle-lamp, which they all flash in gay abandon as we approach.

As a green, wet-behind-the-ears Gang-apprentice, Yours Truly has arrived empty-handed. The others tut scornfully at my lack of Mischief Night tackle, but when we pool all our collective resources, we're just about as well equipped for a session of "mischievin'" as a well-turned out commando unit.

"Reight," says Pongo, assuming overall command of the Unit. "Wheer we offter?"

"On Doggus - ter t'terrace 'ouses. They're closer together, so tha can gerraway easier." This was Danny Parkin, offering his suggestion. He'd obviously given the matter some pre-mission thought the night before.

"Sounds good ter me," affirms Pongo and off we go - along Norristhorpe Lane - "on Doggus".

All the local kids called Norristhorpe "Doggus", so I did the same, without questioning the origin of such an expression. It was only recently that I discovered the quaint derivation of the name. According to local folk-lore, the Lord of the Manor at Liversedge used to keep his hunting dogs in kennels along Norristhorpe Lane, so the area became known as "Doghouse." And there were a few dogs knocking about that dark night in 1958 as the gang made its silent way on to the terrace houses past the end of Liversedge Hall Lane.

Once there, it's time to begin the ritual of a night's "mischievin". As yet, I am completely baffled, by the entire procedure, so I stand back in adolescent admiration while the mischief gets under way. And the first trick is a little beauty.

Puzzling Roy Wetherall's need for a reel of black cotton and Pongo's pride in possessing an envelope full of school drawing pins, I stare in wide-eyed wonder as the prank unfolds before my very eyes. With the instinctive boyhood nose for absolute silence when mischief is afoot, we approach a cobbled back-yard passage-way which divides the rear of the old terrace-houses. The moon gives us sufficient light, so there's no need for give-away torchlight, and Pongo craftily takes out his drawing-pins.

"Reight," he whispers. "Dusta think it's windy enough," he asks no-one in particular.

The others hold up their hands to test the breeze, so I follow suit, embellishing my contribution by wetting my index-finger with spittle and holding it up to assess the wind direction. I am perplexed, but daredn't show myself up by asking the reason for our meteorological activity.

"Aye, Ah reckon it'll do," says Danny.

"Champion," chortles Pongo. "Gerrus some o' yon cotton, Roy." At this, Roy Wetherall breaks off several decent lengths of cotton from his reel.

I remain puzzled as Pongo ties one end of a length first to one drawing-pin and then the other end to another drawing-pin. To the accompaniment of whispered adolescent chuckling and mirth from Danny Parkin and Kipper, this process is repeated several times until Pongo has quite a wad of cotton-connected drawing-pins.

Now, you know how it is when you're thirteen and every

body else about you is laughing, but you know not the source of their mirth. Well, you join in, don't you, to avoid embarrassment? So I chuckled and tittered with the rest, but couldn't for the life of me understand why.

It all became clear very shortly.

After passing a couple of cotton-joined drawing-pins to Kipper, Pongo stealthily makes his way through one of the back-yard gates next to a brick built coal-shed. Slowly, deliberately and in the utmost silence, he creeps up to the curtained back-window of Number Three, and reaches up to the top rail. Holding one of the drawing pins in his left hand, he pins the other to the top rail and gingerly lowers its mate to swing in the gentle night breeze.

A bit further down the said passage-way, Kipper has performed the self-same operation on Number Five. Silently, the pair of miscreants join us at the top of the street.

"Nahthen, just thee watch - only keep reight quiet," instructs Pongo. We all settle down in the shadows to witness the fun.

For a while, the back-street remains eerily silent in the silvery moonlight. The gang remains on radio silence, as instructed, and I am unable to make any pertinent enquiries as to the nature of the "mischief" currently under way. Seeds of doubt as to the sanity of my new-found mates begin to filter their way to the top of my thinking.

"*What are you doing here, crouched down behind this wall in the gloom of a cold November night,*" asks my Inner Voice. I am about to call it a day, and tell these lads what I think of their quaint Yorkshire customs prior to my departure, but before I can utter a word of scorn, the back door of Number Three creaks open. A shaft of light falls across the back-yard.

The silhouette of a burly, waist-coated, stubble-chinned occupant lumbers out into the gloom and calls over his shoulder: "No, there's nob'dy art 'ere tappin' on t'winder, Elsie."

With a huff and a puff, he returns to his evening's tele-viewing, slamming the door behind him.

Behind our wall, we gang members fall about in silent mirth.

Shortly after that, the back door of Number Five opens and the process is repeated, this time by an elderly lady in pinafore and slippers. She too carries on a conversation with someone inside the house.

"Wot d'yer mean, tappin' at back winder, Ernest? There's nob'dy aht 'ere ter do any tappin'. Ah think tha' mus' be 'earin' things." And she, too, departs within, closing the door.

For the next twenty minutes or so, gang members are increasingly silently convulsed, as Numbers Three and Five continue to pop in and out of their back-doors like those male/female weather-indicators some folk used to have on their window-ledges. Surprisingly, none of the victims of the jape bothered to inspect the victimised window in the dark corner of their back-yards. For all I knew, they'd be popping in and out all the live-long night.

Eventually, our laughter turns to boredom, so we leave

them all to it. Silently and stealthily, we creep up the cobbled back-street out onto Norristhorpe Lane, to make our way further "on Doggus".

Our next port of call is another row of terrace houses down by the Rising Sun pub, so a little more stealth and cunning is required if we are to avoid detection. The early-evening drinkers are all hard at it inside, and there's a friendly hum of chatter and the rattle of dominoes from within. But the light from the tap room windows casts too much of a glow onto the Norristhorpe Lane pavement for our liking as we sidle past. We creep across the road and make our way down the back-street of the terrace houses opposite.

"Let's do t'door-knob one," hisses Kipper.

He unslings the washing-line from his shoulder and thrusts it eagerly at Pongo. Kipper is obviously keen to perform this trick as he hops up and down excitedly on the spot. "See - Ah've knotted it already."

He pokes the washing-line under Pongo's nose, revealing that both ends have been tied in loops.

Yours Truly remains puzzled, but if it creates as much mayhem as the previous activity, then I'm all for it. I'm beginning to warm to this Mischief Night business.

"Good idea," whispers Pongo, so the activity is officially sanctioned. "Danny, thee tek one end and Kipper tek t'other, an' let's gerroff ter t'end o' t'street. It'll be quieter darn theer."

And this particular trick turns out to be a little beauty as well...

Down the back-street we creep, keeping low behind the

dividing walls of the back-to-back terraces. The domino rattle and chattering hum from the Rising Sun fades away behind us, and Roy Wetherall whispers to me that the gloom at the bottom of the street is ideal for mischieving activity. We form up outside the very last houses in the row. Beyond us lie the open fields leading "over yonder" - down to Cornmill Lane and Heckmondwike - an excellent getaway route if we should be discovered whilst we're about our dirty trick.

After ascertaining that the curtains of the back-kitchen window are properly drawn, Kipper nips stealthily across the small back-yard of Number Thirty-two. Silently and carefully, he slips the looped end of his washing-line over the brass door knob of the back-door and scuttles away.

Crouching in the shadow of the low back-street wall, the rest of the gang double up in chortles of anticipatory delight. Again, I join in, not knowing the reason why, but fearful of losing face.

"Reight - Ah'm off nar," hisses Danny Parkin, and he creeps across towards the back-yard of the house opposite - Number Thirty-five. Deftly, he trails his end of the rope over the back wall, across the yard and up to Thirty-five's back-door. He waves to Pongo who pulls the rope almost taut and gives Danny the thumbs up.

After carefully knotting the end of the rope round the door-knob of Number Thirty-five, Danny flits silently back to the gang, waiting and chortling in the shadow of the coal-house wall.

So now, unbeknown to the residents, the back-doors of

Numbers Thirty-two and Thirty-five are securely tied together by the Johnson family washing-line.

"Who's offter knock on t'doors, then?" whispers Pongo.

We all look floorwards, avoiding our leader's gaze. Actually knocking on the door is apparently the most dangerous part of the jape. Creeping so close to somebody's back kitchen and pausing long enough to knock on their door represented a definite risk of ear-clouting detection. In addition, the activity just *had* to be synchronised. It was a matter of Life and Death that the raps on both doors were delivered at exactly the same moment, otherwise the game was up.

"Ah dadn't. Ahs'll mek ter much racket wi' these booits on," says Roy Wetherall, and he indicates his stout footwear. Kipper creeps off to the fence near the entrance to the fields, undoing his flies and pulling uncomfortable faces. Danny looks away, rummages through his pockets and begins counting his stock of tupenny cannons.

Pongo's gaze falls expectantly on Yours Truly.

Sensing a heaven-sent opportunity to gain much-needed gang credibility, I pluck up courage and, trembling with fright, I summon up all my adolescent bravado: "Ah'll do it. What dusta want me ter do?"

"Just knock on t'door and then beat it," is Pongo's precise command. "Ah'll do t'other 'un," he nobly volunteers in the true style of Our Revered Leader.

The subsequent few minutes' of adolescent laughter and glee have remained with me throughout my Shoddy Town life. They tickle my ageing ribs even now as I recall the fit of tugging, yanking and adult bawling which followed...

Pongo and I deliver our sharp raps on the back-doors of Numbers Thirty-two and Thirty-five respectively, and sprint for cover by the fence bordering the field.

Number Thirty-two is first to respond. The door opens about five inches and a shaft of light pierces the gloom of the back-yard. There are grunts and exclamations from within as the door, firmly anchored to Number Thirty-five's is wrenched and yanked by the bemused resident.

Meanwhile, Number Thirty-five has responded to Pongo's rap on *their* door. There is a similar series of grunts and calls as the doors are tugged and pulled in unison by their respective owners. As Thirty-two gives his door a hefty pull, so Thirty-five's is torn from his grasp and it slams shut.

"What's goin' on 'ere? Some bugger's pullin' t'door off'n it's 'inges." [Rapid assessment of situation by Number Thirty-five]

"Let go o' mi door-'andle, will yer - 'ooever y'are?" [Thirty-two is slower to cotton on to the current situation]

Over by the fence, the gang of spectators watches. We giggle, titter and chuckle in attempted silent mirth. Eventually, and with little chance of being caught [the victims are imprisoned in their own houses, aren't they?], we laugh out load uproariously as the orgy of yanking and shoving at door-handles continues.

Feeling really brave now, we come out onto the back-street, hooting and jeering derisively. We shriek and yell in adolescent bravado, and point mocking fingers at either side of the street. As Thirty-two's door is pulled back in yet another failed attempt to open it, we encourage Thirty-five: "Goo on, owd lad! Gie it some welly!"

From inside, realisation is beginning to see the light of day: "Yer young buggers! Ahs'll 'ave thee when Ah ger ahtside."

"Thee an' whose army," retorts Pongo, really chancing his arm with youthful cheek. "Tha 'as ter cop us first!"

But before any further banter can take place, a burly, flat-capped figure appears at the top of the back-street, silhouetted against the light of the street-lamp on Norristhorpe Lane. Number Thirty-two has tumbled to what's been going on. He's left their house via his front door onto the next street, chased up onto Norristhorpe Lane and now he's preparing to give chase down their back alley.

Roy is first to spot the impending danger: "Ey up, Pongo! T'mester's 'ere! Let's beat it!"

Laughter and derision ceases abruptly. We all experience that trouser-filling, terror-ridden moment of an impending Caught-in-the-Act nature. But fear not - we have a cunning nearby escape route! In a mad dash of fear-driven flight, we scramble over the fence and through the gate, into the dark safety of the fields above Cornmill Lane, yelling and chortling in our Mischief Night mirth. We sprint away down the slope towards the valley bottom of safety and time gone by.

As I look back over those youthful times, I recall my adolescent enjoyment of our annual "mischieving" feast almost as if I'd been born and bred a Shoddy Town Lad. I well remember the tricks we used to get up to with a certain

"Ahs'll 'ave thee when Ah ger ahtside."

fondness and no mean degree of delight, as gradually I became a *very* experienced mischiever...

One year, we decided to swap all the gates on loose hinges the full length of Lumb Lane. In those days, most of the houses had their numbers on the front gate at the top of the garden path. If we were to swap them all around, in random fashion, wouldn't that be a Mischief Night trick of major proportions? So as soon as a suitable level of darkness had fallen on November 4th that year, our gang of five went about its mischievous business.

No gate with lift-off hinge fixings was safe from Pongo's thoroughly planned mission. Wrought iron gates were the easiest to deal with, since they were lighter and more readily transportable by fourteen year-old lads. We crept up to a front gate and a quick lift upwards was all that was needed to assess its transferability in the half-light of the street-lamp.

If it came off easily, then it would be carted off, silently, as far away up Lumb Lane as possible. Then, it would be re-hung on a similarly vacated opening near the top. The whole enterprise was efficiently directed by Pongo, who had obviously given the matter some thought.

"Oh, Freddie - thee an' Roy tek that un an' purrit up theer, wheer Danny's standin'. An' bring yond darn 'ere ter this un," were his precise instructions which we executed to the letter. But this was one of those tricks which held much more fun in the actual performance than in its effect on the good people of our area.

We chortled and chuckled as we transported the gates the length and breadth of a silent, deserted Lumb Lane; and we fell about in helpless mirth as we hung them on completely the wrong gate-openings. But at that point, the fun petered out.

All that was left to us was the contemplation of tomorrow morning's perplexed postman. We pictured his dilemma as he attempted to deliver his sackful of GPO material, scratching his head and trotting up and down in search of the correctly numbered houses.

In those days, the GPO, who ran the telephone system, were also an unwitting source of Mischief Night fun.

Armed with a pocketful of tanners, you could have half-an-hour's worth of mischief at the telephone box on Huddersfield Road, just above the Yew Tree pub. For Yours Truly, it turned out to be a bit expensive, though, when I weighed it up against my half-a-crown earnings from my Saturday job at Sydney Clarke's Florists, so the popularity of this particular prank was often economically driven. If we hadn't enough "brass", then the trick was a non-starter.

But this year, our pockets fairly bulge with tanners.

After a session of running away from the irate residents of "Doggus", we've re-convened for further mischief outside the said telephone-box. Needless to say, it is Pongo who organises proceedings.

He's taken out the blue-covered telephone directory, which was always provided on a low shelf in those big red telephone boxes of yester-year, and he holds it an angle to catch the light of the street-lamp. Nonchalantly thumbing through the lists of names and numbers, he eventually makes an executive decision.

"Reight! We's'll do this un 'ere," and he reads out the name of our randomly selected victim. "'*Hawksworth, P. W., Chapel Fold, Cleckheaton.*' They'll do."

After reciting the number out loud in order to commit it to memory, he inserts his chubby fingers into the dial-holes on the silvery wheel of the telephone - and off we go...

Sometimes, when you got through to your victim, as selected by Pongo's Random Choice method, it was a simple matter of yelling down the phone: "Gerroff the line, there's a train comin'," and slamming the phone down immediately. It wasn't a bad sixpenny trick and we often managed a tanner's worth of giggles out of it.

On other occasions, our trick required a little more stage-management. We'd wedge open the heavy, multi-glass panelled door of the telephone box with our bodies, and practise making farmyard animal noises around the receiver. After we'd established our confidence in producing the said sound-effect, one of us would make the call.

The sixpenny piece clatters down into the grey box, and, to a background of baaing and mooing, Mischief Night caller announces: "Ah'm callin' from Baildon an' Ah'm stuck at t'side o' t'road wi' nowheer ter gooa."

He'd hold out the receiver towards us and we'd continue our farmyard impressions until the pips went.

But eventually, anxious to see value for money in the Mischief Night hoax stakes, we became a little more adventurous. Admittedly, the price of the trick was doubled - from a tanner to a bob - but it was worth the gamble in our mischievous adolescent eyes...

Pongo selects our next victim from the directory: "Nahthen, let's 'ave a see ... 'Ere we are: '*Longbottom, H.T., Walkley Villas, Heckmondwike*'. Reight, Danny, get thi brass ready".

Danny Parkin, son of a local Headmaster, is charged with responsibility for the next two or three minutes' worth of fun. Danny has the gift of the gab, and he can turn on a posh accent at the drop of a hat, so he is ideally equipped for playing this prank.

Unwittingly, the GPO have played right into our Mischief Night hands by abandoning the Button A/ Button B* system some while before. Once you're through, press your tanner into the slot, and off you go. No need to worry about Button A for connection or Button B for the return of your hard-earned cash.

Once again, we wedge open the heavy door of the telephone box with our bodies, and crowd round Danny in the booth. He places his row of tanners on the top of the metal phone-box in front of him and clears his throat. It takes Kipper a full minute to stop hopping up and down in excited antici-pation but eventually, we all fall silent in expectant mirth.

Danny picks up the receiver and dials the number, as instructed. When he hears the call answered, he rams in his sixpence and announces, in a plummy, official-sounding voice: "Good evening. This is the GPO here. We'd just like to test the quality of your telephone-line."

*Button A/Button B   a method of making calls from old-
                      fashioned telephone-boxes
                      See "Up the Snicket" pp 9-11

"Could you have a bucket of water ready to immerse your receiver, in about five minutes' time, please? Our engineer will ring you back in about five minutes. Thank you."

And he hangs up.

Now what today's reader of this particular Shoddy Town tale must realise is that these are the care-free times before the modern-day, incessant flow of cold calls to the home telephone. The days of the double-glazing offer and the star-prize holiday call were yet to dawn. Thus, unsuspecting victims of our Mischief Night hoaxes would often readily agree to carry out bizarre tasks, believing that Danny was actually a GPO engineer, proceeding about his standard, technological business of customer service.

Our strike rate was probably about one in five. We were prepared to lose upwards of a couple of shillings on calls which resulted in a typical Shoddy Town response of: "Bugger off, yer cheeky young sod," or "Tha must think Ah cem up t'river on an old steam-booat, yer daft little 'aporth."

But on this occasion, our 5-1 bet has paid off.

We ring back [at additional cost!] and sure enough, H.T. Longbottom of Walkley Villas has filled his bucket and is waiting beside the phone.

"Now you'll hear a high-pitched tone," says Danny in his plummy voice. "When you hear this, please immerse your receiver in the bucket of water, walk ten feet away, and shout back to us if you can still hear the tone."

H.T. Longbottom readily agrees, whereupon Danny performs a very credible impression of a high-pitched factory-whistle about six feet away from the receiver. The rest of us double up in fits of youthful laughter. We split our collective sides at the thought of a submerged telephone in Heckmondwike and a very attentive GPO customer, straining his ears to catch the sound of Danny's high-pitched whistle from ten feet down the hallway...

There were variations to Danny's pretend GPO engineer instructions.

On some occasions, after his initial formal greeting, he might instruct the customer to stand six feet from the phone and whistle; or turn off all the lights and shout; or go out into the garden and stand on one leg. Nearly all of his instructions had successful Mischief Night outcomes at one time or another, and the results gave us hours of side-splitting laughter for weeks afterwards...

From this side of the rose-coloured spectacles of Time-Gone-By, I fondly recall serving my Mischief Night apprenticeship. The tricks we played were outrageously naughty in their day, and if we'd ever been caught, we'd have been for a very lofty high-jump, both at home and at school. But we never did get caught out, each one of us experiencing the soaring adrenalin rush as we chased away from the scene of our Mischief Night crimes, calling out over our shoulders to any would-be pursuer: "Tha's ter cop me first, yer daft old sod!"

Today, forty-odd years on, Mischief Night appears to have blended in to an all-year-round travesty of vandalism and damage to property. The once-a-year "naughty-for-a-night" festival of impudence and fun seems to have lost its appeal for today's youngsters, and those yester-year tricks of ours have become tame and perhaps, unexciting.

Despite all that, those 1950's pranks have become deeply embedded in my Shoddy Town identity. After all, it took me a great deal of time, effort and courage to become an accomplished, accredited Mischiever. Even today, at my ripe old age, come the afternoon of November 4th, I still feel the adrenalin charge of delightful naughtiness on those dark evenings of Long-Ago.

Nowadays, my own personal Shoddy Town history has produced a suspicious mind, so at 6.30pm on Mischief Night each year, I look out of our front window in the desperate hope of catching some modern-day mischievers about their naughty business. But they are nowhere to be seen.

The street is dark, empty and silent.

Disappointed, I feel the need to liven up the evening, as in days of yore. Turning my back on the Present, I drift away to the Yew Tree telephone box and round the corner "on Doggus".

I rummage about in my yester-year pockets. Now where did I put those drawing-pins and that black thread. And have I got a pocketful of tanners...?

***

A BIT OF A LAD

By the time I was twelve, I'd begun to think that I belonged to a family of gypsies, albeit without a caravan or a horse.

As recounted elsewhere in these Shoddy Town tales, my early life was notable for the regularity with which my family upped sticks and moved to another part of the country, where my Dad had found himself a better job. By the summer of 1957, he had managed to find better jobs in Nottingham [where I was born], Wolverhampton [where I started school], Peterborough [where the countryside was very flat], Stroud [where the people were all yonderly rural] and The Heavy Woollen District [which became my adopted, permanent home].

I didn't realise the effect all this itinerant behaviour had had on me until I'd reached my early twenties, and I displayed an active resistance to travelling any great distances - even to go on my holidays. The back garden was fine for my summer vacations, thank you very much.

However, back in 1957, after settling in West Yorkshire, finding educational provision at Batley Grammar School and learning to wear a very thick vest in winter, I began to seek identity as a proper Shoddy Town Lad. *This* was my new home; *this* was where I was going to stay; and, most important of all, *this* was where I longed to belong.

Now, most of the lads I met at school had been born and

bred in the Batley/Birstall area, so their dynasties stretched back into the deep, historical roots of the shoddy trade. In terms of pedigree, the best I could offer was a Scotswoman for a mother, a Nottinghamshire moulder for a father, and a life-long supportership of Notts County - the oldest Football League club in the World.

Such biographical facts paled into insignificance alongside those of Mike North, Jack Hirst, Haydn Mitchell and Malcolm Charlesworth - all of whom were natives of God's Own County and to whom I looked up with admiration. So I set about building an identity for myself which would become accepted amongst my Shoddy Town peers...

Now, you know how it is, don't you? You've overcome the first effects of being a complete outsider at school by adopting a mode of speech which enables you to be accepted by your new mates and to fend off the school bullies. Your scholastic performance in 2Alpha at Batley Grammar School identifies you as being middle of the class - neither a "numpty" nor [far more importantly] a "swot". You're a reasonable footballer and cricketer, on the verge of selection for the school teams. So where do you go from here?

The answer to that vexing question lay in the sub-culture of that 1950's Grammar School. You had to be daring enough for all your mates to admire your bravado. You had to be cheeky enough to get into minor trouble whilst you were in school, and you had to perform lots of "no-no's" when you were out of it.

And in those far-off days, did I play to the crowd!

As a result, my antics earned me quite a few Saturday

Morning detentions for minor BGS offences, all of which helped to establish my reputation as a bit of a lad.

Talking after the dinner-bell in the dining-room; failing to get $^7/_{10}$ for Mr Bumstead's History tests; being late back to school at dinner-time [because I'd been smoking on the Mud Bath]; giggling with Pip Whitehead in Screwy Lewy's Chemistry class. All these insignificant misdemeanours earned me a BGS-committed Saturday morning. But far more importantly, my mates began to admire my cheek and bravado. I became accepted as a bit of a naughty boy - one of the [Shoddy Town] lads.

Sporting prowess went hand-in-hand with acceptance into the ranks of The-Lads-That-Mattered Crew. I'd recently been selected to play for the school football team, thereby adding even more creditworthiness to my reputation. All matches took place on Saturday mornings but, needless to say, at BGS, discipline came first. Any boy receiving a detention was automatically dropped from the side, his Saturday morning was to be spent in purgatory, and decisions about his selection for the following week were left in abeyance.

I well recall my feelings of inner anguish as I drop my pencil in one of Bumstead's History lessons. The echoes of its clatter on the wooden classroom floor have hardly faded away as the master gleefully delivers his crippling sentence:

"Ah ha! Butler! One dropped pencil! Saturday morning detention for you, my boy..."

So now I sit, my sullen head bowed, elbows resting on one of the long, oak desks in the Geography Room as my two hour detention commences. Befitting the BGS tradition, Bumstead has set me an essay on "The Inventions of the Industrial Revolution" to be completed during my two hours' purgatory.

Along with a dozen or so other miscreants, I set to in the bright spring-time silence of a March Saturday morning.

But that silence is soon shattered by the outside chatter of boys and the clatter of studs on concrete. Looking out of the big classroom window, I can vividly recall my utter despair as I witness my team-mates in their dark blue/light-blue shirts spilling gleefully out of the changing-rooms oppo-site. Unseen by the master in charge, they laugh and point at me in my BGS prison-cell.

Haydn Mitchell and Roy Pollard turn half-way up the driveway slope and flick derisory, two-fingered gestures at me, chortling and ridiculing my present plight. They make their happy way up onto the top cinder-track and out onto Carlinghow Hill. In five minutes' time, they'll be cavorting around the Billiard Table, relishing every second of their ninety minutes' sporting fun.

But I'm condemned to two hours of History.

My abiding memory of that particular detention [and several others during my Grammar School career], is hearing the distant calls and shouts of my mates at about 11am as they returned along the cinder-track. Fresh from their endeavours in the name of Batley Grammar School, streaked with glorious Billiard Table mud, they perform an encore of their two-fingered gestures as they pass the huge Geography Room window. Desperate to know the score, I gaze longingly after them at the changing-room doors.

I hope they have lost heavily, having had to manage an entire game without *my* stalwart defensive qualities.

But overall, what I remember most vividly about those awful Saturday Mornings is the discipline-reinforcement technique adopted by the masters in charge of the detention.

Having spent the last two hours writing a fairly decent [albeit punitive] piece of prose, as indicated by the subject teacher, I would down pen in joyful relief at the end of my period of sentence. But before release into the freedom and sunshine of the week-end, I must present my work for inspection...

We miserable miscreants form a line and proceed to hand in our two hours' worth of academic toil. The master casts a cursory glance over my three or four foolscap sides of written work and nods his satisfaction that I haven't been doodling idly for the last two hours. Then, almost spitefully, he smiles at me and tears the sheets in two before languidly tossing the pieces into the nearby waste-paper basket.

All that work - for nothing! My period of purgatory is complete...

Of course, all information regarding Saturday Morning detentions had to be kept completely secret from my Mum and Dad. If I were to return home from school at any time with the startling news that I'd been given a detention, then I'd receive further vexation as a result of domestic parental discipline which would take the form of a sound, rhythmic thrashing. *That* was definitely out of the question, so I invented a desperate tactic to avoid detection. Whenever I was awarded a Saturday Morning detention, I said absolutely nothing about it to either of my parents. I'd cunningly avoid all conversations regarding the coming Saturday morning's activities until my Dad asked the inevitable question towards the fag-end of the school week: "Playing football tomorrer morning, are yer?"

"'Course Ah am," I'd fib. "We're at 'ome agen 'Eckmondwike. Ah'm playin' Right Back," and I'd dash upstairs to pack my kit.

Saturday morning, bright and early, I'd wave a cheery "goodbye" to Mum and make my way down to the Bar House to catch the big, red number 20 bus [Mirfield-Leeds, via Batley]. In my bag, I'd have my Manfield Hotspur football boots, my dark blue/light blue school shirt and my white shorts. Secretly tucked underneath all that sporting gear would be the real equipment for this particular BGS Saturday morning - a selection of pens and my box of "Oxford" mathematical instruments...

After completing my two hours' penal servitude, I'd make my dismal return home at about mid-day. Alighting the bus at the Bar House, instead of making a dash up the road for our house, I'd nip round the corner to the patch of grass outside the shop. Surreptitiously removing my football shorts and shirt, I'd rub them in the muddy grass. If there was a puddle or two about, I'd give my boots a good soaking, too. It was only then that I'd make my way home.

Entering the house and whistling artificially cheerfully, I'd announce to my Mum that we'd beaten Heckmondwike Grammar School 3-0 and that I had been Man-of-the-Match. I'd receive her congratulations as I unpacked my filthy kit, to all appearances, only recently involved in youthfully robust soccer action, such was its dirty condition.

By the time the long summer holidays of 1959 were over and I was making my way up Carlinghow Hill for life anew in 4Alpha, I was beginning to be hailed by all The BGS Shoddy Town Lads-That-Mattered as a genuine, fifteen year-old "lad" in the true grammar school tradition.

But that Autumn term of 1959 turned out to be a pretty disastrous affair for Yours Truly, as recorded in my BGS School Report Book, which lies before me on the desk at this very moment...

The faded blue cover carries the simple title:

BATLEY
GRAMMAR SCHOOL
Founded 1612

Inside, on the first page, is the school crest with its pompous Latin motto: *Forte Non Ignave*, followed on the next page by my biographical details, completed in my Mum's own neat hand.

Flicking idly through the double pages for 1957 and 1958, all of which record a fairly successful academic settling-in period, my now-ageing finger comes to rest on the Headmaster's summary of my performance during the Autumn Term, 1959. Signed *F.W.Scott*, it reads: "*I trust he has learned his lesson.*" And the memories come flooding back...

In the early months of that year, it had become a matter of creeping suspicion in the Butler household that their elder son had begun to sample the delights of tobacco. But the careful reader of these tales will already have noted that I'd actually begun to use the vile weed at a much younger age, after relieving telephone boxes of their loose change in the summer of 1953.

Nevertheless, my tobacco habit had remained dormant until my arrival at BGS and with it, the need to prove my naughtiness to my newly-acquired Shoddy Town chums. And even though my Dad smoked Player's Medium Navy Cut with avid enthusiasm, the practice was *absolutely* forbidden territory to his two sons. Being caught meant either a sound rhythmic thrashing and a week of early bed-times, or the denial of weekly spending money - the vital wherewithal for the purchase of the diabolical weeds!

So both my brother, Robin, and I ensured complete secrecy at all times in smoking-related matters - until that night in February, 1959. On a fairly breezy evening, I made my usual 7 o'clock announcement to Mum and Dad:

"Ah'm just off dahn to t'Bar House for some spogs."

"Speak properly," scolds my Mum, noting my Shoddy Town imitation accent.

"Very well, Mother," I reply, obsequiously. I am desperate to get out of the house for a much-needed nicotine-intake, and I make for the glass-panelled back door before any further discussion regarding my mode of speech can be undertaken.

Along our short drive I dash, out onto the pavement of the main Huddersfield Road and down past Roy Wetherall's house. I sprint like a man possessed, as far as the old whale-bone arch under the trees, about a hundred yards up the road from the Bar House shop. There I pull up and dive into my pocket for my Woodbine packet and its only remaining "Great Little Cigarette".

Shielding the bright golden flame of my match from the stiff breeze, I suck furiously on the little white pleasure-stick. I inhale deeply and at last, I am at peace with the world. A smile of adolescent satisfaction lights my face in the darkness and I complete my journey to the Bar House at a leisurely stroll.

Minutes later, I descend the steep stone steps outside the shop having completed my transaction with Mrs Mitton. I have successfully replenished my Woodbine stocks for tomorrow with five more of the "Great Little Cigarettes", along with a quarter of dolly mixtures to hand round upon my return home. For my Mum and Dad, this will verify the need for my recent trip to the shop.

Once I am outside on the pavement, I realise that the freedom to smoke will last but a few minutes longer [a mere three hundred yards up the road to our house]. Urgently, I light up another cigarette, and begin my last leisurely stroll of the evening.

Reaching our gate with a goodly proportion of my cigarette yet to be consumed, I reject the idea of discarding 60% of a good smoke in the hedge bottom. With bare-faced cheek, I open the metal gate and begin my walk down our short drive. Mum and Dad are well-ensconced in their arm-chairs in the back room, aren't they? They are far too engrossed in their evening's tele-viewing to be bothered about their elder son walking down the driveway, "Woodie" in hand.

Brazenly, I walk right up to our glass-panelled back door

and mount the steps, live smoking equipment still between my fingers. I take one last pull on the Great Little Cigarette and deftly nip off the burning end. Nonchalantly, I flick the "tab" away, towards the back garden.

At this very moment, the stiff breeze picks up the brightly glowing ember of my fag-end and whisks it back towards me. I duck as it flies past, across the panes of the glass-panelled door in front of me, and on into oblivion up our drive.

Craftily, I pop a Polo mint into my mouth to disguise my tobacco-reeking exhalations and casually reach for the door-handle. Whistling an appropriately cheerful tune, I walk into the hallway - to be confronted by the glowering figure of my Dad.

Removing a half-smoked Players' Medium Navy Cut from the corner of his mouth, he stands for a second or two in seething silence. With a sinister, "I-am-about-to-deliver-a-thrashing" edge to his voice, he states: "You've bin smokin', 'aven't yer?"

By this time in my short life, I have become adept at assessing a disciplinary situation such as this for possible impending physical harm. I enter Risk Assessment Mode* and make a hasty decision to lie.

"What? Me? Smokin'? No, never..."

But I have been betrayed by the wayward breeze, the glowing red-end of a discarded fag, and the fact that most of the glass used in 1950's windows was two-way and thus, very definitely, see-through.

*See "Down the Ginnel" "Living with the truth" p 40

After carefully extinguishing his cigarette in a nearby kitchen ash-tray, Dad delivers a sound, rythmical thrashing and despatches me up the little wooden staircase to bed. For a week or two, I am almost *persona non grata* in our Huddersfield Road house as a dark shadow of guilt hangs over me. I carry the mark of Cain - A Smoker, at fourteen years of age

But then, one night in early March, events take a somewhat poetic turn. Unbeknown t o Yours Truly, just before retiring at precisely 10.30pm in preparation for the coming day's foundry toil, my Dad smokes the very last fag in his packet of Players' Medium Navy Cut.

The following morning, at precisely 6.59am, I am fast asleep. At 7.00am, I stir from my slumber and, in the thin dawn light of my bedroom, I observe an adult shape bending over my dressing table where I store tomorrow's little schoolboy pile of things for my pocket. The shape desperately rifles through my belongings - loose change, handkerchief, pen, pencils. With its nose not three inches away from the dressing-table top in the early-morning half-light, it is urgently searching for something.

Eventually, with a little cluck of gleeful delight, the shape removes a Great Little Cigarette from my packet of five, holds it up for inspection in the early-morning bedroom gloom, and retreats warily through the door.

That "shape" had been my Dad in the throes of post-breakfast nicotine cravings. He had been desperate for a smoke of any kind, so he had come to raid my erstwhile secret supply of Woodbines. As a result, for a few weeks at any rate, the shadow of guilt gradually drifts away into a bright, sunlit, clear blue sky. I settle down to bask in the smug glow of parental approval for a while, my smoking habit conveniently ignored. But just as I feel that the hurdle has been successfully cleared, there is a hitch. It occurs in late April as the 1958-59 football season is drawing to a close.

Earlier that year, on a February half-term morning, sitting round the smouldering embers of our fire down at the old derelict house just off Roberttown Lane, our Huddersfield Road gang comprising Jack "Pongo" Dixon, Roy Wetherall, Sam "Kipper" Johnson and Danny Parkin, passed a resolution to form a football team. If we could manage to rope in six other, unsuspecting local lads, all us founder members of the team would be guaranteed a game.

Yours Truly receives such an idea with exultant enthusiasm. I am in the last throes of my Gang-stipulated Apprenticeship, almost an accepted *bona-fide* Shoddy Town lad. A successful debut as a decent footballer would just about complete my probationary period, and I'd become one of the lads.

Now, our gang of five represented four different local schools, and since the majority of us weren't regular members of our respective school teams, the idea of self-selection was very appealing. Smiles of smug satisfaction lit each of our five faces as we contemplated the idea of playing in precisely the position of our choice. For myself, I was going to be a world-class centre-forward, scoring goals a-plenty and celebrating with a Denis Law-style raised arm.

Having between us a catchment area for players which stretched from Cleckheaton in the West to Batley in the

East, we set about our recruitment drive for extra player-members with avid enthusiasm. To cut a long story down a bit, by the middle of March, after many rash promises about playing conditions, kit and facilities, we'd pulled in the required six kids from the surrounding districts.

Using his eloquent and silky tones, persuasive Danny Parkin managed to strike an equipment deal with Ronnie Robinson, an ex-Huddersfield Town player who ran a sports shop in Heckmondwike. Further to the purchase of a new football, Ronnie loaned us a brand-new set of white, blue-hooped "continental" shirts to be paid for at a later date: "When tha gets on thi feet, lads. Best o' luck ter yer..."

We are over the moon. Now we're all kitted out and in possession of a brand new ball, and we're raring to go. But there remains one of the most pressing of all Association Football problems: We'd nowhere and nobody to play.

At a team executive meeting down our cellar at 166 Huddersfield Road, we scratch our heads and wrack our brains for a solution to our dilemma. There were plenty of local Under-18 League teams, but at our age, we didn't relish the thought of facing up to the hard men of junior football in such outlandish venues as Firthcliffe, Chickenley or Ravensthorpe. Those players would eat us alive, to say nothing of their spectators. Local rumour was rife that, at Firthcliffe in particular, both right and left wingers from visiting teams were always in imminent danger of having a bike chucked at them as they wove their silky dribbling skills down their respective touchlines.

Our meeting closed with no positive resolution passed.

Several days later, a jubilant Pongo calls another meeting.

He has found a solution to our problematic lack of suitable opposition. His Heckmondwike Grammar School mate is forming a team up Howden Clough at Birstall and they, too, are in our position. At break-time that day, Pongo had struck a deal and a fixture had been organised for a Monday afternoon in the approaching Easter holidays: Howden Clough United v. Huddersfield Road Wanderers.

"We've ter be on t'council field up Birstall - opposite t'White 'Oss pub, half-two, Monday," is Pongo's succinct summary of arrangements.

We are overjoyed. At last, a game presented us with the opportunity for extremely selfish team selection. At the end of the following ten minutes, Yours Truly has entered his name on the team-sheet at centre-forward, despite being classified at BGS as a stodgy full-back on the fringes of the school Under-15 XI.

The Easter holiday passes agonisingly slowly, but before too long, we are alighting from the rear-platform of the HWD Transport Company omnibus on Leeds Road at Howden Clough, just outside The White Horse public house. We're about an hour-and-a-half in advance of the arranged kick-off time, so there are no members of the opposition around to greet our arrival.

We make our way up the steps alongside the high wall at the side of the main road. The pitch is large and flat, so we begin to relish the thought of our impending game. Across the field, behind a low fence, lie the council estate houses from whence our opposition will no doubt emerge in about three-quarters of an hour's time. We rub our hands in anticipatory glee, inspect both goal-mouths, walk round the pitch a couple of times - and then adolescent boredom sets in.

"Oh," says Pongo, looking across at The White Horse pub. "What sez we nip in fer a pint afore t'game, then?"

This suggestion receives a mixed reaction from the team.

"What? Suppin' afore a game? Tha mus' be off thi chump, Pongo. It'd mek thi dizzy on t'field o' play." This is sensible Danny Parkin, ridiculing the notion.

"Tha'd be slashin' all through t'game if tha does," advises Roy Wetherall whose much older brother David had obviously warned him in advance about the effects of alcohol on the human constitution.

"Ah'm not allowed," fibs Kipper, seeking to save adolescent face. "Mi mother sez it's ner good fer thi spots."

For myself, I'm not so sure. I knew the intake of alcohol was *absolutely* forbidden in our house. I also knew that its consumption was for adults only, but I was also familiar with snatches of overheard conversations amongst the Big Lads at BGS. They often bragged about going "to t'Anchor" or "t'Black Tulip dahn Dewsbury on a Sat'day neet." And these self-same Big Lads commanded our BGS respect for such acts of defiant bravado.

In addition, going in to the White Horse with Pongo for pre-match refreshment would represent the crowning touch to my Gang-stipulated Apprenticeship, wouldn't it? Such an act of daring adult defiance would score highly on the "One of the Lads" qualifications criteria-list. And I'd be accepted by all and sundry as a genuine Shoddy Town lad.

Throwing caution to the wind, I buck the current trend of reluctance. "Reight, Pongo," I enthuse. "Lerrus gerrin fer a pint, then." And I make my braggart way down the steps onto the road.

The others remain on the field, observing our awesome swagger as we cross the road. I pause at the foot of the grey stone steps leading in to the gloomy interior of the ale-house. Only recently installed in long-trousers, I rummage in my pockets for my packet of Woodbines. Pongo, who is hot on my heels, stumbles into me and we halt on the pavement.

" 'Ere," I say, proffering a cigarette. "It'd bi best if we leet up. Then we's'll look reight," I state knowingly.

Pongo agrees and takes the freely awarded Woodbine. For the briefest of moments while he is lighting up, I feel a sense of misgiving. What we are about to do is *seriously naughty* and, if discovered, will incur the horrendously ferocious wrath of both my Mum and Dad.

I hesitate as a mental picture of my trilbied Dad glowers forbiddingly at me from somewhere in the ether above my head. But the thought-bubble bursts in a surge of adrenalin-rush and I push open the Tap Room door...

Inside The White Horse Tap Room, there is little activity this particular lunch-time. The high windows of the Victorian ale-house allow little light, so the dim lamps in the ceiling are in day-time use. Their wan glow falls across a couple of flat-capped, overalled figures standing in a dark corner, enjoying a lunch-time pint.

They turn and raise mildly enquiring eyebrows as Pongo and I amble nonchalantly to the bar. Our hands are deep in our pockets and we puff in manly fashion on our Woodies.

A middle-aged, balding barman eyes us up and down without saying a word.

I stroll up to the bar, brimming with youthful confidence, and place a care-free left boot on the shiny brass foot-rail. I open my mouth to speak - and I'm completely taken aback.

Never having been in this position before in all my fourteen years, I am utterly nonplussed as to how to actually ask for beer in a pub. A wave of panic seizes me, but before I can begin any inept, give-away mumbling request, Pongo steps forward.

"Two gills o'bitter, landlord," he demands authoritatively.

I am speechless with admiration for Pongo's obvious familiarity with the technicalities of pub jargon. He winks at me knowingly as the barman nods silently and begins pulling two halves of Bentley's Yorkshire Bitter into straight half-pint glasses. He takes them out from beneath the porcelain-handled draught pumps and places them, dripping and brim full, on a brass bar-tray in front of us. Narrowing his eyes somewhat suspiciously, I thought, he demands his payment: "That'll bi one an' a tanner, lads. Thankin' you."

"We've done it," I think to myself. *"We've been served in a pub and nobody's asked any questions."* I relish the thought of my next BGS play-time, bragging about this to an attentive crowd of Mud Bath mates.

But, let's be honest. That first taste of what will, in time, become the amber Nectar of the Gods, is the very embodiment of foulness itself! Pongo and I purse our lips and draw in our cheeks as the first wave of BYB hits our taste buds.

"Two gills o'bitter, landlord."

We daredn't express our disgust, however, pretending, as we were, to be hardened drinkers of some years' experience. We smoke our Woodbines with carefree nonchalance as we take in the drab surroundings of the gloomy taproom, pulling secret faces of disgust as the bitter liquid hits the pits of our stomachs .

Ten minutes and four brave gulps later, we're out on the street, staving off attacks of beer-invoked nausea. "Bloody 'ell! That wor rammy stuff. It must 'a' bin off," groans Pongo, clutching his belly.

"Yer," I nod in sympathy. "Ah dooan't know what they see in it. Ah think Ah'm offter bi sick somewheer."

I rush across the road and up the steps to the side of the Howden Clough football pitch where the rest of the team await our return. They stare at us in adolescent admiration.

"What y'ad," enquires Kipper reverentially.

Staving off the gips from the pit of my stomach and acting like a man, I am the big, bold braggart. I lie through gritted teeth: " 'Alf o' bitter. It wor real, man! Tha owt ter a' come wi' us."

A shout from the council houses across the opposite side of the pitch halts further enquiries and it's not long before we take to the field of play in our brand new kit. The historic first-ever game involving Huddersfield Road Wanderers and Howden Clough United kicks off at precisely 2.30pm, as arranged...

A six-nil thrashing and a bus ride later, I make my way up our drive - the Wanderer returned. I still harbour a need to be sick after my lunch-time libation but daredn't refuse the gargantuan steak pie and mashed potato tea which has been lovingly prepared by my Mum.

The clock ticks round to ten past five and in comes my Dad, fresh from his labours at P & C Garnett's Cleckheaton foundry. He bursts into our kitchen where the evening repast awaits, but he is in no mood for eating.

Hardly has his trilby left his head for the hallway hat-stand than he launches into a fearsome tirade: "Yer young bogger," he growls at me, and advances menacingly towards my side of the small kitchen-table. "Yer've bin drinkin' this afternoon, 'aven't yer?"

I am utterly flabbergasted. How can he have known? Cleckheaton is many miles from Howden Clough. Whilst I was in the tap room of the White Horse, Dad *must* have been supervising the tapping-out of the furnace, staring conscientiously at a couple of tons of white-hot metal as Tommy Ancliffe poured it from the huge crane-slung ladle into the waiting moulds. So I know for a fact that Dad hadn't been at our game to witness my initiation into the ranks of alcohol-consumers nor, for that matter, my beer-affected performance on the football field.

I decide to enter Risk Assessment phase and begin to fashion a huge lie.

I adopt a greatly-offended, protestation show of innocence. "Me? Drinkin'? This afternoon? Am Ah 'earin' yer reight, Dad? Ah've 'ad a sup o' tea after t'game', if that's what tha means."

"Speak properly," admonishes my Mother, whereupon, for safety's sake, I abandon the Shoddy Town mode of speech.

"I can't think who would have told you such a thing, father. I've been playing football at Howden Clough."

"And yer've been into a pub," continues my Dad. "An' Ah'll tell yer who told me. It wor Billy Ramsbottom. 'E'd bin 'ome for 'is dinner and 'e'd missed 'is bus back. 'E told me all about you and that Jack Dixon when 'e got back to work, just before we tapped out. Ah'll let daylight through yer, yer little bogger."

Well, the game was up.

Without waiting to hear any evidence for the defence of Me, sentence is passed. Dad launches into a fierce, rhythmic thrashing. I am soundly beaten about the body in staccato rhythm, all the way upstairs to my bedroom where I am banished, without nourishment, for the rest of the evening.

Payment of my "spend" is cancelled forthwith and I am forbidden to associate with any members of our gang. Furthermore, the only time I am allowed to leave the house is to continue with my part-time job at Sidney Clarke's, the florist/market-gardener down Huddersfield Road. Such activity at least guarantees me a weekly stipend of half-a-crown and enables me to maintain my daily stocks of Woodbines for consumption off the premises.

For another period of indefinite duration, I am once again *persona non grata* in our Huddersfield Road house as that black cloud of shameful guilt lands on my shoulders. The mark of Cain is now double-stamped - A Smoker *and* A Drinker, at fourteen years of age.

Things cannot get much worse. Every waking moment for

the next week or two, I receive black looks of the "shame-on-the-family-name" sort. I am not allowed out of the house for fear of meeting up with "that Jack Dixon", and my list of weekly household chores expands considerably...

As the weeks pass, however, I gradually manage to wheedle my way back into the Butler family favour. Passing an internal vow never to be a naughty boy ever again, I display an almost obsequious willingness to carry out my punitive tasks without the usual adolescent moaning and groaning. By the end of the summer holidays, I have managed to salvage some of my family reputation and I become "normal" again. I am even allowed out to mix with the members of the Huddersfield Road Wanderers football team.

Later in the year, my fifteenth birthday passes and - joy of joys - I receive official recognition of my Huddersfield Road Gang Apprenticeship.

Now in the Fourth Year at BGS, I am accepted at school as a genuine Shoddy Town Lad, so there is little need for adolescent bravado in the search for approval amongst my contemporaries. I receive fewer and fewer Saturday mornings, play more and more regularly for the school football team, and even begin to make progress with my academic studies.

And then, one November Saturday night, out on the town in Heckmondwike, the dark of the Palace cinema becomes yet another scene of my adolescent demise...

Following my re-instatement as a well-behaved family-member, largely as a result of my improved scholastic performance at Batley, my Mum and Dad had allowed me a bit of free rein to wander with my Huddersfield Road chums. This meant that I'd developed the Saturday night habit of going to the pictures with one or two mates for a spot of media entertainment.

It required stumping up threepence bus-fare to travel down to the centre of Heckmondwike, along with the surrender of one and sixpence to the managements of either The Palace or The Pavilion Cinemas. This came pretty steep out of your half-crown pocket money, but for a couple of hours' worth of celluloid entertainment, it was worth it.

I became quite a regular attender at The Palace in particular. I'd only recently completed a period of courtship with a lass from Heckmondwike Grammar School which saw me forking out three bob for a double seat and a two-hour ration of darkness. Her aunty was one of the usherettes who lit the way to your seat with a big shiny torch, so she'd soon tired of having her courting activities supervised from a distance by an eagle-eyed member of her family. She'd given me the push in favour of an older lad who'd promised to take her to The Pioneers in Dewsbury, which was way beyond my fifteen year-old wallet.

But despite Cupid's Wayward Dart, I'd continued The Palace habit, forgoing the pleasure of female company for that of my mates. But I am still well enough known there for the lady in the kiosk and the usherette to pass a Saturday night "Hello, luv," as I receive my pink-coloured ticket at the kiosk before disappearing into the gloom inside.

So on the Saturday night I'm talking about, four or five of us had made our noisy way past the Market Place clock, down Croft Street to the cinema entrance. Into the warmth of The Palace we'd dashed, regardless of the film currently on offer. Our mission objective is the safe-haven of darkness in which to perpetrate minor acts of adolescent mischief.

Now and again, during the quietest moment of a passionate love-scene, Pongo would pluck up enough courage to slide low in his seat and give out with a pre-conceived cat-call: "Gerroff an' milk it!"

The resultant peal of laughter which ran round the auditorium would have the usherettes and Mr Manager scuttling about in the dark, flashing their torches at all and sundry in the effort to discover the owner of the disruptive fog-horn voice. But it was to no avail.

By the time they shone their torches at us, we were all sitting quietly, outwardly attentive, watching the screen, inwardly chortling with schoolboy glee. And we'd keep up the act until the torches were switched off and the officials in charge returned to their stations at the back of the cinema.

One of the best of such remarks which leaps out of the mists of time was perpetrated by Roy Wetherall during a tense moment in the film "Dracula". Just as Christopher Lee is poised to plunge his glistening fangs into the silky white neck of his latest victim, Roy lets out with: "Fancy a drink, lass?"

The drama of the moment is lost and the Heckmondwike audience collapses in fits of laughter. The beams of search-light torches thrash about the rows of seats in a frenzied search for the miscreant, but as usual, in our row, they pick out only avid, attentive film-watchers.

Tonight, the film is a particularly tedious affair. Opportune cat-call moments are few and far between, so we turn to other activities for our Saturday evening's entertainment...

At the end of our row of seats, Sammy "Kipper" Johnson is lost in the film, despite its boring effect on the rest of us. He is a film buff *par excellence*, preferring to lose himself in the magic of the silver screen rather than to join in with our childish pranks. He sits, captivated and lost in tonight's offering from the Hollywood Dream Factory.

Pongo's exciting activity for this evening is cunningly simple, and he whispers his intent to the rest of us: "Ah'm off on t'row ter swipe Kipper's shoelaces while 'e's watchin' film." He ducks down into the darkness and squirms his way to the end of the row.

In seconds, he is back, brandishing Kipper's shoelaces above his head for all to see.

We giggle in silent mirth, look furtively at Kipper who continues to gaze obliviously in awesome wonder at the silver screen, and applaud Pongo's cheek. In seconds, however, the trick is over and done with, and we seek further entertainment.

Indolently, and in the safety of the darkness, Roy Wetherall leans back in his seat, strikes a match and lights up a cigarette. With the glint of naughtiness in his eye, Pongo mischievously proffers the end of one of Kipper's shoe laces and nods knowingly at Roy. The tip of the flame is held below the shoe-lace which was once Kipper's and within seconds, it is burning brightly.

The rest of us are convulsed with laughter at the craziness of Pongo's trick. We roll about in our seats, clutching our sides in helpless fits of fairly quiet mirth. The orange radiance casts a bright glow around our row of seats and, as the shoe-lace continues to burn, so its beacon-like qualities increase. It is just about to shout to the manager and the usherettes: "Hey! Look over here! Some youngsters playing pranks," when Pongo realises the give-away nature of the burning shoe-lace's beacon-like glow. He blows desperately on it in an effort to extinguish the leaping flames, but this only serves to fan them into brighter, even more tell-tale light.

With an increasing sense of panic, he attempts to spit on the flames in an effort to douse them with human water. This ploy fails miserably and Pongo's panic increases in proportion to the flames' leaping incendiary qualities.

In a final, desperate attempt to avoid detection by The Palace authorities, he flings the lighted bootlace forward three or four rows and dives for cover beneath his seat. The glowing material that was once Kipper's shoe-lace has become a virtual comet-tail as it arcs its parabola through the cinema darkness.

People in the front rows leap from their seats and begin shouting abusively. As the projectile lands in Row Seven, one old chap grabs his flat cap and sets about beating out the flames.

An usherette has now arrived on the scene, hot-foot from the rear of the cinema auditorium where she was about to strap on her ice-cream tray full of goodies for the interval. A tarty-looking woman in a fur-coat begins the process of our eviction by identifying Pongo as the culprit of this latest jape:

"It wor that little sod! 'Im over yonder." And she points an accusing finger in the general direction of our row.

The piercing beam of the usherette's torch singles out Roy Wetherall who has by now ceased his fits of mirth and is white-faced at the prospect of being caught.

Roy stands and manfully attempts to deny any involvement: "Tha wot? Me? Shoe-laces? Setting fire to shoe-laces? Ah dooan't know what tha'r on abaht, missis."

But the game is yet again up. Mr Manager is called and he strides down the aisle towards our row. Brooking no nonsense of any kind, he delivers his professional assessment of the situation.

"Tha could 'a' set all t'place a-fire, yer daft little sods." And he gives us our marching orders. "Reight! All t'lot on yer! OUT! NOW!"

Up to this point, Kipper has remained totally engrossed in the film. He is startled by Mr Manager's vehement tone and is taken aback: "What? Me an' all, mister? But Ah's'll miss t'end o' t'film."

He receives short shrift from the navy-suited Mr Manager. "Tha should 'a' thowt o' that afore tha started messin' abaht, shouldn't yer?"

By now, several Saturday night film-goers have had their entertainment interrupted enough to turn and remonstrate with we noise-makers. Several usherettes have joined the fray as well and there is a frenzy of accusations and flashing torches. One of the usherettes is that afore-mentioned lass's aunty, so *my* goose is well and truly cooked.

"Well, Fred Butler!" she scolds. "Fancy you causing bother! I wouldn't 'ave thought it..." And she shakes her head disparagingly.

In the last throes of adolescent protestations of innocence, and maintaining his wounded-pride attitude to the last, Danny Parkin goes a little too far: "Burr Ah've done nowt to be thrown out for," he whines. And then in a more confidential tone: "If Ah've to go out, can Ah 'ave mi brass back, mister?"

This is the straw to break Mr Manager's dorsal bit. In the glow of the torches, we catch sight of his crimson cheeks as he prepares for another onslaught of admonishment. But he doesn't get the chance, for we sense that the affair is over. We silently file out of the row, up the aisle to the rear doors.

There are many tuts of disgust from the cashier in the kiosk as she peers at us over her half-moon spectacles. "Disgusting little gutter-snipes," she calls after us as we traipse down the steps.

Outside on the pavement, it is Gang Recrimination Time: "Yer daft sod, Pongo," whines Kipper. "What did yer do that for? Ah wor reight enjoyin' that picture."

"That's cost me one and six, Pongo - an' Ah aven't 'ad mi ice-cream," moans Roy Wetherall. "Ah wor reight lookin' forrard to it ."

" 'An Ah 'ad ter dock mi cig aht when t'manager came," I complain vociferously. "It wor mi last 'un an' all." And I stalk angrily off up the street alongside the red-brick wall of The Palace towards the Market Place.

Inwardly seething and bitter about the loss of my last Woodbine, I leave the rest of the gang behind. In a fit of disgust, I decide to make my way to the bus-stop and head for home - alone.

Now, at such a point in this particular Shoddy Town tale, we step into the realms of conjecture, guesswork and gossip.

Yours Truly is no longer present outside The Palace Cinema with the rest of the Huddersfield Road gang. They are dawdling way behind me in the shadows, along the cinema wall, laughing and joking as they recount the evening's events thus far. As they reach the large fire-exit doors of The Palace, I am well on my angry way along Westgate towards the bus-stop beside the central municipal gardens - known locally as "The Green". So what follows is based on adolescent hearsay and Shoddy Town myth...

Still brimming with indignation, the Gang *may* have decided to exact revenge on the Palace management. On the other hand, a dire constitutional need *may* have arisen amongst several gang members. And this desire *may* have occurred in each of them all at the same instant. But to this day, History has never yielded the name of the person who presented the subsequent action-plan to the gang for collective consideration.

It turned out to be simple enough in its execution. One of the lads [or it may have been all of them, for all I knew] decided to answer the call of nature up against the said fire-door. Whether this was done silently or celebrated raucously in brash adolescent defiance, Yours Truly will never know.

All that is certain is that a considerable quantity of still-warm-and-steaming wee is discovered by Mr Extremely Irate Manager, minutes after our eviction from the cinema. He stands and fumes as a river of liquid runs down his maroon-coloured fire-door, meanders across the pavement like the mighty Mississippi before gurgling below ground down a nearby Croft Street drain.

Meanwhile, I have boarded the number 19 HWD Omnibus opposite Gooder's Plumbers' shop on Greenside. I present my threepence fare to the blue-uniformed conductor, but lacking any tobacco requisites for my smoking pleasure, I angrily take a seat on the lower deck.

I return home quite early from my Saturday evening "on the town", much to the surprise of my Mum and Dad. " T'film wor rubbish," I mutter as I shed my trendy black three-quarter-length overcoat.

"Speak properly," scolds my mother, failing to realise that my ill-will has been brought on by the effects of nicotine-deprivation.

"Right," I retort. "I'm off to bed then. Goodnight."

My Dad raises his eyebrows at my early departure for the Land of Nod, but says nothing. Our Robin is similarly taken aback, because it means that he, too, must now make the trip up the little wooden staircase to accompany me. Together, we silently make our ways upstairs, and my week-end's excitement peters out like a damp squib...

The following Monday morning finds me earnestly engaged in Charlie Spurr's ten o'clock Maths lesson. As I chew the end of my pencil and desperately ponder the complexities of the Sine Rule, there is a knock on the classroom door of 4alpha. A prefect enters and enquires of Mr Spurr if the boy Butler can go immediately to the Headmaster's office.

My mates look at me with some degree of adolescent

admiration. A summons to the Boss's Office can only mean that I'm in trouble. I begin to quake inwardly, for what reason, as yet, I know not.

All the way down the wide staircase onto the lower floor, I wrack my brains to discover the reason for my summons. It has been some while since I've been detained at BGS's pleasure on a Saturday Morning, so it can't be my absence from detention which has prompted this call. Neither have I been caught smoking on the Mud Bath...

Traipsing miserably along the wooden-panelled corridor of the lower floor, I continue to ponder.

My behaviour towards the lasses from the Girls' Grammar School in the bus station after school has been nothing less than chivalrous, so it can't be that. Neither have I misbehaved on the big red Number 20 HWD Transport Company Omnibus on the way home. By the time I reach the Head's Office, I am completely nonplussed as to what it is that I've done wrong.

I stand in trembling fright outside the Boss's Office, the huge oak door of which is tight shut. I daredn't knock, so I stand, waiting for my knees to stop crashing fearfully into each other.

"Come in, Butler," booms F.W.Scott from within.

"*Bloody 'ell*," exclaims my Inner Voice in Shoddy Town Speak. " *'E can see through t'door baht openin' it.*"

All of us at BGS lived in fear of ex-Army officer Francis Willoughby Scott whose be-gowned appearance and piercing eyes struck us dumb with incomprehensible terror. His strange, ex-Army ways were frightening in their unfamiliarity to us Batley lads, and we respected them through a mixture of raw fear and an adolescent lack of understanding.

The awesome power of F.W.'s ability to see through solid wooden doors increases my sense of terrified reverence as I enter the inner sanctum. Now, like a frightened rabbit caught in the headlight beam, I stand before him, trans-fixed.

He eyes me up and down in sinister silence.

After what seems an age, his rasping, staccato delivery rocks me back onto my fifteen year-old heels: "So you pee on cinema doors on Saturday nights in Heckmondwike, do you?"

For a moment, I endeavour to establish my astronomical position. I am caught in a time-warp between Monday morning near the top of Carlinghow Hill, Batley [Now], and Saturday evening at the bottom of Croft Street in Heckmondwike [Then]. In the far reaches of my mind, I struggle to comprehend my current situation.

"*How the Hell does he know you've been down Heckmondwike on Saturday night. And what on Earth is he talking about peeing on doors for,*" queries my Inner Voice, speaking properly now, because it knows we're in trouble.

Outwardly, I am a mumbling wreck, so my everyday voice comes up with a pathetic: "I don't know, sir."

F.W. hoists himself up to full height, expands his thoracic cavity to maximum cubic capacity, and proceeds to boom at me from a distance of all of three feet: "You don't know? You *don't* know? You go to the pictures on Saturday night and proceed to drag the excellent name of this school down to the level of the gutter - by being ejected? Who were you with, eh?"

"I... er ... I don't know, sir..." My voice trails away into a whimper. F.W. knows all the answers already, it seems, so why waste time asking me all these questions?

"You don't know? You *don't* know? So who went out onto the street and peed on the cinema door, eh?"

"I...er...I don't know, sir." My reply to this particular enquiry was indeed the honest-to-goodness truth.

F.W. fixes me with that piercing eye and delivers his verdict: "You will go home now and you will return with your father. We shall then discuss your future at this school. Go!"

He waves an imperious hand in the direction of the door, turns his begowned back on me and proceeds to rifle through some papers on his desk...

At an uncharacteristically early hour, I return home to face the wrath and tears of my mother. At mid-day, I am once again beaten rhythmically by my father and dismissed to bed for the rest of the day. All the way up the little wooden staircase, words like *shame, disgrace, disgust* and *dishonour* are slung like barbs at me and I spend the next few days in forced withdrawal from society.

A couple of mornings later, I have to accompany my Dad to school, where the whole incident is re-examined in F.W.Scott's office.

There is a great deal of discussion about the extremely good name of the school having been desecrated forever in the surrounding district, and the subject of urination on exterior woodwork is given a thorough airing.

At no point is my part in the said action examined by anybody. I am presumed guilty as charged and I bow my head in anticipation of the hanging, drawing and quartering which I am certain will inevitably follow.

With his foundryman's trilby clasped reverentially in front of him, my Dad uses the word "sir" a great deal and is forced to plead for a continuation of my Batley Grammar School status. F.W. resorts to a great deal of military terminology as he alternately berates me and laments the outstanding reputation of the school being hauled through the Shoddy Town mire.

I stand, head bowed and take it all on the chin. I begin to contemplate life at Healey Boys' School which is where I am certain to end up, but as the steam-valve of F.W.'s anger gradually slides shut, both adults are suitably convinced about my repentance and I am dismissed sternly to my class.

During the ensuing private conversation, he enlightens my Dad as to the nature of his Saturday Night Intelligence-Gathering Service. It becomes clear that the aunty of the lass I used to be friendly with had shopped me to Mr Manager of the cinema. I was the only one whom she had recognised out of our Huddersfield Road gang. As a result, Mr Extremely Irate Manager, hopping mad at the desecra-tion of his cinema building, had telephoned BGS first thing on Monday morning to provide F.W. Scott with the full low-down on my week-end activities.

For yet another, even longer period, I am once again

persona non grata in our Huddersfield Road house. An increasing number of those dark shadows of shameful guilt land heavily on my shoulders. The mark of Cain is now treble-stamped - A Smoker, A Drinker *and* A Urinater, at fifteeen...

There is little I can do about the situation. To vehemently declare my innocence in the matter of my urinary misbehaviour would, in 1959, have been tantamount to a full and frank confession of guilt. So I said nothing and took what was coming to me.

Out of normal school hours, I was house-bound for several weeks. I was, however, allowed to continue my weekly Saturday morning travail at Sydney Clarke's, thus again allowing for tobacco-stock replacement. But beyond that, I had to stay indoors every night and endure the stony stares of punitive parental retribution. Both my Mum and my Dad sat in forbidding silence as they stared at the twelve-inch television screen in front of them, completely ignoring my presence altogether.

When the story finally broke amongst the lads at BGS, I was severely mocked by some of the Sixth Form Prefects. Whenever I passed by, they made piddling gestures up against playground walls, grovelling at their flies. And they cat-called at me across crowded corridors: "Oh, Butler! Dusta fancy a piss, then? Just gerron wi' it, lad."

All the kids around me would hoot in derisive laughter.

But the whole affair was a seven-day wonder and my wayward behaviour on that Saturday night forty-odd years ago was soon forgotten. I had, however, earned quite a reputation amongst The Lads-that-Mattered Crew. My daring feat of defiance and my supposed gesture against authority [and the cinema wall] earned me a good deal of respect. My credit-record throughout the school as a genuine Shoddy Town Lad lasted for quite a time - long enough, in fact to fend off any bullying by Big Bad 5B lads until, at long last, I too reached their Big Lad status...

So now it's time to shelve that old, blue-covered report book, but not before I take a last, rueful look of regret at F.W.Scott's entry for 1959: *"I trust he has learned his lesson."*

With a sigh, I turn the page to 1960, and a smile of satisfaction begins to light my wrinkled old face.

By then, I'd managed to shake off the "bit of a lad" label and my Form Master, P.B.["Pobble"] Enfield has written in glowing terms:

> *"He has been a sound deputy form captain*
> *and has worked well to establish himself*
> *as a reliable member of the form."*

The Headmaster's summary for that year, however, remains dismissively blank.

But I *have* learned my lesson, sir! I have, indeed - with particular regard to cinema fire- doors.

***

THE GIFT  OF A VOICE

Being a "comer-in" to Yorkshire, I've always thought that you have to have a very loud voice as part and parcel of your basic qualifications for becoming a *bona fide* Shoddy Town Lad. I came to this conclusion in 1958, when I finally settled in at Batley Grammar School from the depths of Cider-with-Rosie country. At that time, or so it seemed to me, all the big lads could shout the length of the Mud Bath or across the front yard, in order to gain attention or to enforce their oft-perverted will.

You were left in no doubt when you were singled out during a morning play-time by a Big Bad 5B lad with stubbly chin and meaningful glare. He was on a desperate search for a nicotine infusion, so you were button-holed for inquisition: "Oh, thee, young 'un! 'As ta any cigs on thi?"

Those stentorian tones would boom across the playground, rattling classroom windows in their casements and vibrating door-handles loose from their fixings. You knew you'd been pin-pointed as the centre of attention because the wave of sound would shake the fillings loose in your teeth. Everybody else around you only felt the slightest of tremors in theirs.

So now, in quaking fear of the Big Bad 5B lad, it was time to whisper your response in the form of a bald lie.

"Ave Ah 'ell. Ah'm nooan one o' t'bacca party..."

If you were lucky you'd escape a body-search, but a further booming address would follow, delivered at maximum decibels for the benefit of all youngsters who were listening: "Well, tha'd best get some tomorrer, owd cock, else Ahs'll bray thi 'eead off o' t'top o' t'wall if tha dunt..."

I marvelled at the influence wielded by the possessor of such a powerful voice and vowed that when I got to be a Big Lad in three or four years time, I would cultivate the same skill. So I grew through the BGS ranks, developing and nurturing a fog-horn voice which was the playground envy of my mates.

I learned to yell the length of the back field: "Oh, Mitch! Aster dun thi Maths 'omework?"

This overt and noisy communication-technique ensured an embarrassed reply from Our Hero who found himself flushed out into the open regarding academic work. Not daring to show himself up by admitting that he'd actually completed the said homework the night before, properly, like a Good Little Swot, he would shout in like vein:

"'Ave Ah chuff! Ah'm offter copy it off Pearsall."

I soon discovered that making loud noises at the top of my not-insubstantial voice ensured my relative safety from collective sarcasm and ridicule. Nobody had a loud enough voice to return the challenge, so I remained safe in my cocoon of noisy behaviour, didn't I?

But it wasn't always for my own benefit that I employed my God-given gift. Being of a socialist nature at heart, I would often use my powers for the benefit of others...

It's 10.45am on a sunny spring morning on the Mud Bath - a

vast overgrown tract of land opposite the front entrance of BGS, bounded by large hawthorn bushes. A steady column of lads of varying ages traipses, soldier-like, across the road and through the gate, keeping to the left along the top boundary. They're making their solemn, ritualistic way up the line for a smoke.

In the shadow of a particularly large, thorny bush which we'd nick-named "The Docker* Tree", we would gather round for a whiff or two of Wild Woodbine, Player's Medium or Senior Service. As we relished our fifteen minutes' respite from lessons, the air would be blue with vivid Shoddy Town invective and tobacco clouds. And when we'd finished our smokes, we used to fasten the tab-ends onto an available spike on the said hawthorn bush, so that, in time, it became festooned with white tobacco stubs. Often, from afar, locals out with their dogs would marvel at one bush which maintained a full flush of white blossom throughout the year, regardless of season.

Forty-five years on, I revel now in the memory of those fifteen-minute morning rituals of nicotine intake. Out of sight of the prying masters, who were all doing the same in the warm comfort of their staff room, we puffed away the happy hours of our Shoddy Town youth.

At the time, being caught meant instant dismissal from the ranks of the grammar school and expulsion to Healey Boys' School or anywhere else they'd take you on. So preservation of status was vitally important. This meant mounting

*Docker   the last vestiges of a smoked untipped cigarette, usually about $1/4$in long, if you'd remembered to bring your pin to school that morning.

an effective and far-seeing guard during all such Rest and Recuperation Bacca Party Sorties.

And who better than someone with a fog-horn voice which could be heard from miles away - even on busy Bradford Road down in the valley below? Yes, the post of Look Out often fell to Yours Truly because I had the most effective warning device in my larynx.

Picture the scene: A crowd of Big Lads huddles beneath the Docker Tree, enveloped in a cloud of communally friendly smoke. A few yards away, in the knee-high, wispy bracken of the Mud Bath, stands Yours Truly, relishing every last drag of my ever-shortening Woodbine, but keeping a wary weather-eye out for any sign of officialdom.

From the far end of the field, having just left the track leading from Field Hill via the Mud Bath back to BGS, the school-capped heads of a column of First Year kids hove into sight. This is the Baths Class, making its way back for lessons after a session with Harold Blackburn, moustachioed resident Swimming Coach at Batley Baths, near the top of Cambridge Street.

For their morning's activity so far, these First Year kids have been cajoled, exhorted and shouted at to swim back and forth across the width of the baths. Most have them have spent the entire lesson in mortal dread of their Coach.

Now, anybody who has been in the BGS ranks for any length of time will vividly recall Harold Blackburn's coaching technique. Suitably clad in white shirt, grey trousers and white plimsolls, he was an advocate of the Fiercely Vociferous Instruction technique for the aquatic education of many generations of young Batley lads.

Leaning and straining over the edge of the big pool, Mr Blackburn would tower above us and yell at the top of his voice: "Now, laddie, DO IT AGAIN - only this time - BREATHE!"

The echoes of his terror-inducing instructions would raise a tidal wave of sonic boom across the baths, all but washing away the more slightly built lads in the form. He frightened me out of my Shoddy Town trunks as I turned tail with the rest of the class and fled, desperately breast-stroking my way to the far side and temporary shelter from Mr Blackburn's vociferous ballistic blasting. We all swam as if our lives depended on it, out of our collective desire for personal survival.

He was still at it, years later, when I finally took up my first teaching job at Batley Boys' High School. But in 1967, I was able to sit in a nearby cubicle and watch the Master perform his aquatic magic on my young charges, fearful now that some of them might drown in the tidal wave produced by his still-mighty vocal attacks...

However, on this particular spring day in 1962, most of those afore-mentioned BGS nippers were relieved to be marching, crocodile-fashion, back to school. Some of them had been so frightened out of their First Year wits by the yelled instructions of the Coach that the water around them had turned a murky shade of urinary amber as they'd floundered and thrashed their way across the bath.

But now they are dry and safe and on their way back to school. They are all knackered, but they have to endure the long, short-trousered trek across the Market Place, down

Branch Road, over Bradford Road, up Field Hill and across the Mud Bath to school. After a forty minute soaking in the icy waters of the baths, their little white knees are turning a bright blue in the crisp morning air. Frost-bite and exposure have begun to set in, and they begin to dawdle, dragging their eleven year-old tired little heels.

The master in charge of the expedition must exhort the stragglers or they'll be late for the next lesson. On this occasion, the accompanying master is Brian "Basher" Smith, Head of PE and Borough Road trained - a fitness fanatic and sworn enemy of Woodbines, Player's Medium and Senior Service. He strides to the head of the queue and issues a traditional BGS threat to the young column of kids:

"Any boy who is late for the next lesson will receive a Saturday Morning detention."

The response is immediate. Lingering symptoms of frost-bite vanish; colour returns to pale, wan cheeks; exhausted legs become charged with youthful energy. The column heads for school, rejuvenated by the threat of a BGS committed Saturday morning.

As Basher's raven-haired napper bobs into sight above the rise next to the railway-line fence in the far corner of the Mud Bath, I turn to my tobacco-enriched colleagues in a bit of a panic. If he so much as catches a whiff of nicotine on the clear morning air, Mr Smith will have us expelled for sure. It is imperative that I give a warning to my chums.

I fill my lungs to capacity and, in a naturally-produced and utterly wholesome bellow, I drown out the whistle of the passing Coddy Bob steam-train on its way down the line to Batley station: "Ey up! There's Basher! Dock 'em, lads!"

The Mud Bath resounds to a sonic boom of Harold Blackburn proportions as I employ my natural fog-horn to good socialist effect. My chums are suitably alerted.

In a frenzy of incendiary extinguishing, the Bacca Party rid themselves of any potentially incriminating evidence and we all adopt nonchalant play-time poses. Jock Sawdon sprawls indolently on the sparse Mud Bath grass, hands behind his head. Jim Flexney strolls back and forth, whistling "Lipstick on your Collar". Yours Truly walks off, eyes skywards, looking for all the world like an avid bird-watcher seeking a sighting of the rare Mud Bath Golden Eagle.

If Basher sniffs the slightest whiff of a Woodbine on the clear Mud Bath air, we shall be noted in his little green book and Healey Boys' School will be our educational environment for the remainder of our time at school. But the Butler Bellow has achieved the desired effect.

The Baths Party crocodiles its way past and Basher fixes us with a wry, meaningful stare. As soon as he has passed from view, beyond the bushes and through the gate onto Carlinghow Hill, we re-light our dockers and settle back for a hassle-free "bacca session". Once again, we are enveloped in a cloud of communally friendly smoke...

But the possession of a fog-horn voice was not all beer-and-skittles. There were times when my brash, loud, Shoddy Town tones landed me in red-faced embarrassment. On such occasions, I often regretted the natural attribute in question and wished that I'd learned to keep my Shoddy Town mouth tightly shut.

Around the football fields of the 1960's West Riding, a

God-given fog-horn was a definite advantage in playing the Beautiful Game.

For instance, you could warn your fellow defenders of imminent danger in the penalty area; or indicate to your team-mates your immediate intentions in the current game; or encourage other players in your team to find available spaces on the field of play where their skills could be of best advantage to your side's performance. As Big Jack Charlton told us during those winter-time coaching sessions: "Ye's need ter pley fudball wi' yer mooths as much as yer feet, boys."

I took this advice from the Great Man to heart.

I would spend entire Saturday mornings shouting my head off for the benefit of the BGS First Eleven, often to no material effect whatsoever on either performances or results . Undaunted, I would take to the field in the old gold and black shirt of P&C Garnett's works team in the Spen Valley League the same afternoon, and do likewise all over again. The end results were probably about the same in both cases.

I would return home that evening, absolutely knackered. This was as a result of my hugely vociferous contributions to a game rather than because of my physical participation in the form of running, kicking and tackling. I began to wonder if it was worth the expenditure of all that vocal energy, since results on the field weren't all that impressive. But I never *really* learned to keep my mouth shut, even though there were many times when remaining silent would have saved enormous quantities of face...

My Most Embarrassing Moment occurred in the twilight

years of my playing days on Soldiers Fields in Leeds, one bright, sunny afternoon in March, 1973.

I'd been playing for a couple of seasons for Leeds Academicals Third XI in Division Three of the Yorkshire Old Boys' League. The principal reason for so doing was that Earlsheaton School colleagues could play together in the same side. Along with Norman Owen, Steve Jackson and Alan Hepworth [a Life-Long Shoddy Town friend], I would grace the green sward with my unfettered fog-horn, bellowing in joyful abandon as the Saturday afternoons passed in long hours of post-adolescent fun.

On the occasion I'm talking about, we were playing against a Barclay's Bank side who favoured the Long Ball, [Route One] tactic to pressure our defence. We were being held together by the sterling efforts of Alan Hepworth, playing today as sweeper to my centre-half rôle.

Stocky, stalwart, ex-miner Alan was a classy footballer who was on his way out of the game having reached an age when gardening and bird-watching had begun to seem far more attractive than cavorting around the football fields of the North. He'd been a First Teamer of note some years before, and had retained those enviable skills as the years had marched on.

Today, his considerable defensive qualities were being called into play on a regular basis.

The Bank's tactics were simple: Goalkeeper whacks the ball as high as possible towards our goal and ten members of his side make a bee-line for our penalty area. Wave after wave of white-shirted Barclay's Bank lads charge at us down the field, each beady, financial eye fixed firmly and meaningfully on our 'keeper. As yet, they have met with little success. In fact, with the ball-playing skills of Steve Jackson and Norman Owen, we're beginning to make inroads into their defence...

Another of our piercing attacks is warded off by the Bank's defence and their goalkeeper prepares to launch yet one more towering clearance to pierce ours. I am fully aware of the consequences of such an action, and I prepare to bring my headgear into operation.

The 'keeper kicks the ball as high as he possibly can and their beefy forwards tear down the considerable slope of Soldier's Fields Pitch Number 7b to bear down on our goal.

The ball disappears into the bright sunlight, launched into the oblivion of the skies above Leeds. Undaunted, I bring my tactical fog-horn into play.

"My ball, Alan! This is mine! Leave it, Alan!"

Such is the sonic quality of my call that many players on several of the adjacent pitches [all called Alan, no doubt] stop and turn, believing themselves to be the object of my playing instructions. Our game-ball is still somewhere high in the stratosphere as I begin my leap to head clear, still shouting the while to audibly underline my instruction: "Right, Alan! Leave this to me!"

I leap, stag-like, still unaware of the ball's precise location in its passage to Earth. During my upwards trajectory, I am still bellowing and waving my arms about in dramatic tactical gestures.

As a result, the games on those nearby pitches have now temporarily halted to witness my majestic bound skywards and subsequent powerful header. Many players and referees, too, stand with hands on hips in sporting anticipation.

I re-emphasise my instructions in fog-horn fashion: My ball, Alan! Leave it, Al!"

But at the very summit of my flight, I catch sight of the ball high above me, and realise that it is well over my head. In a trice, I change tack:

"Your ball, Alan," and I fall to Earth in a collapsed heap of failed ambition.

Laughter peals from the surrounding pitches and the referees announce the end of the temporary halt to their particular games. I clamber to my feet, the colour of beetroot as the contingent twenty-two on our pitch [including my own team-mates] hoot their derision.

Alan, taken completely off-guard by my sudden mid-air change of tactics, has reacted amazingly swiftly for a player of his advancing years. He deftly and decisively clears the ball with a hefty boot into touch.

"Thanks for the early warning," he grins as he trots away.

The whole incident is relegated to talking-point status in the various pubs of the district, long after the last strains of final whistles have faded away on the evening breeze...

Now, you'd think that the ownership of a booming, stentorian voice would be a decided attribute in my chosen career as a teacher - and you'd be right.

Early on in my time at Batley Boys' High School, I discovered that I could transcend the noisiest of adolescent rabbles in classroom or playground with a few well-chosen clarion-calls [the trademark of any member of the profession]. The old hands at Batley High were quick to offer their advice about the effects of a strident shout of a naughty boy's name, yelled out pointedly above the chaotic rabble of my early attempts at teaching Form 9.

The technique was a guaranteed attention-grabber. I was able to command at least thirty seconds' worth of undivided concentration from my unruly charges by the use of the carefully phrased yell. Coupled with some threat of imminent danger, you had to name a specific boy in your quest for disciplinary control:

"POPPLE! Are you tired of livin' lad?"

Or:

"ROBERTSHAW! Isn't it time you got yourself fettled?"

The effect was magical and instant. A silence would fall on the assembled gathering and all eyes in the class would fall on the named person. With bated breath they would await the named one's fate.

In the ensuing silence I was able to give at least a couple of instructions before the rabble once again raised the roof...

But the echo of the most memorable of such disciplinary interjections still resounds across the thirty-five years since my early teaching career began. It was uttered one summer morning in 1969 by my afore-mentioned footballing chum, Norman Owen, a huge, square-jawed teacher of Outdoor Pursuits at Earlsheaton Secondary School.

Amiable and sympathetic, short-back-and-sides Norman always seemed to end up with several classes of often disaffected naughty boys and girls, but he took them all in his well-meaning stride.

On this particular occasion, I happened to pass his open classroom door as he was settling his class of Fourth Years to the daily classroom grind. Attempting to establish start-of-lesson control over the class of noisy fifteen year-olds, Norman cleared his mighty throat and delivered a classic disciplinary clarion-call:

"See! HALSTEAD! Sit DOWN lad, afore Ah knock thi DOWN!"

The disciplinary effect on the entire group was magical and immediate...

At about this time, I discovered that, besides being a definite attribute in your collection of pre-requisite teaching skills, a set of case-hardened vocal chords had other, quite pleasurable side-benefits as well.

Having been encouraged to take up thespian activities by Geoff Holmes - Head of English at Earlsheaton and long-haired leading light in the Dewsbury Arts Group of the early 1970's - I discovered the art of coarse acting. My booming voice enabled me to perform fairly adequately on the huge stage that was a feature of the school at that time. Set in the depths of a vast auditorium, the cavernous stage demanded a klaxon-like amount of volume from the aspiring, would-be actor if he was to be heard by anyone sitting beyond row four in the Hall.

And I had volume a-plenty - with some to spare!

As time progressed, I found producers at the Arts Group were eager to press for my services in many minor rôles, particularly those with a military flavour. My huge boom was readily tailored to fit the requirements of several sergeant-major parts by a succession of skillful producers. Moreover, the more elderly members of our Arts Group audiences relished in the fact that they could hear very nicely, thank you very much, every single word of the dialogue that I managed to remember and/or to deliver correctly.

But it all came to a seriously fearful climax in the open-air summer of 1972, in front of a crowd of some 2000 local folk...

As usual, the Arts Group had been invited to perform in the Quarry Theatre at the House of the Resurrection on Commemoration Day. This was a prestigious annual event at the Church of England Retreat in Mirfield [not quite a Shoddy Town, but near enough] and it was attended by crowds from far and near.

For we budding thespians, it was a feather in our acting caps to be asked to participate in the production. Rehearsals took place on balmy summer evenings in the open-air Quarry Theatre, overlooking the main road out to Brighouse, devoid now of seriously heavy traffic in the hush of the evening. The perk was that we were revered and regaled by the incumbents of the House, all of whom regarded us as "luvvies" with special dispensation because we were assisting in the Commemoration Day celebrations.

On the occasion I'm talking about, my booming tones had been ear-marked by producer Russell Whiteley to play the part of a Roman centurion at the foot of Our Lord's cross, in a play entitled "The Day's Beginning". I was instructed to play the rôle as a barking sergeant-major with the voice of a fog-horn.

I was beginning to think that my parts were becoming stereo-typed.

Only twelve months previously, I'd played in "Androcles and the Lion" at the self-same celebration. Then, I'd been cast as a Roman centurion - a barking sergeant-major type with the voice of a fog-horn. Shouting orders and insults at Archie Madden [playing Androcles] was a comic delight, but, in the open-air of the Quarry Theatre, it required exercise of the vocal chords of heroic proportions - and I was the man for the job.

Playing the cameo-rôle of sergeant-major in a stereo-typed Cockney twang, I'd swaggered the dusty, open-air stage, employing every morsel of my God-given sonic boom to reach the back-rows, up in the sky far above us. The effect on my speaking equipment had been negligible, but I did find myself relishing in those quiet classroom moments during the day when all the kids in the class were writing. Vocal input from their teacher was not immediately required and I took every pleasure from those infrequent periods of Rest and Recuperation for my oral apparatus...

And this year, on a fairly breezy summer's afternoon in "The Day's Beginning", I swaggered my Cockney swagger all over again, perhaps this time, straining my larynx even harder in the effort to reach those folk sitting high in the "gods".

The performances passed successfully. We received our plaudits from an appreciative audience, went for our traditional supper with the inmates of the House and eventually bade them a thespian farewell until the following year.

And that, you might think, was that. Well it was, except that now, during my daily travail as a teacher, I kept having to clear my voice in order to project my erstwhile powerful sonic blast. My ability to transcend most scholastic noise with my shouting equipment was called into serious question - and I began to fear the worst.

The most important tool in my teacher's box of gear - my powerful voice - was failing me on a daily basis. Kids took no notice of me in corridors, in the playground and on the football field. It was almost as if I wasn't there as I attempted to deliver my trademark sonic boom, only to come up with a pathetic little squeak. I began to think that my teaching career was at an end. Drastic action *had* to be taken.

Off I pop to my local GP who refers me to Mr Ghandi, a specialist at Staincliffe Hospital - atop the hill, overlooking the mills and factories of Shoddy Town Dewsbury.

By now, I am somewhat afraid.

During my Shoddy Town life, as has been recorded throughout these tales, I have been partial to the odd Woodbine or two. The effects of such diabolical weeds on lungs and voices is well-documented, so at that time in my teaching life, I began to think dark thoughts about the failures of my voice-box.

Had the regular intake of Wild Woodbine smoke finally taken its malicious toll? Was I a goner?

Now, the only way these questions are going to be answered, is by allowing someone in the know about such matters to have a look. But how do you look at a voice? You can't take it out and lay it on the desk in front of the surgeon:

"There y'are, Doctor. What dusta think ter that, then?"

And he doesn't once it over, circulate the table, poke at it with his pencil and marvel at it: "By Gow, Fred, lad! It's a bloody beauty is yond, an' no mistake!"

But Mr Ghandi soon dispelled all such layman's concerns.

Yes, he was going to inspect my vocal chords. Yes, he was going to shine a light down my throat. And yes, he would establish the cause of the trouble - with a little bit of flat wood, rather like those spoons we used to get with our tubs of ice cream from the sweetie shop when we were kids.

This wiry, precise little man with his white surgeon's coat and a round reflective disc mounted on his head was going to answer all my unanswered questions in one go - *with an ice-cream spoon*?

"Now. Mr Butler...Please open your mouth extremely widely."

I comply readily, leaning my head back and presenting the surgeon with a gob-opening of cavernous proportions. Mr Ghandi switches on the light in his head-gear, almost dives in to my oral chasm, and thrusts the wooden spoon to the very nether reaches at the back of my tongue.

With this latter move, my larynx is extremely displeased. Mustering an involuntary contraction [known in Shoddy Town speak as a "gip"], it hurtles the wooden spoon back towards its owner with, I have to say, some force. But Mr

Ghandi is not dismayed. According to him, this is a very common occurrence, so he continues his quest down the back of my throat for a further ten minutes or so.

Each time he pokes the wooden spoon down my oral cavity, my larynx fires it back at him with increasing velocity. Wooden spoons fly all over the place and we lose two or three of them behind cupboards and in the corners of the consulting room before Mr Ghandi sighs frustratedly. "You have a very sensitive larynx, Mr Butler. I am indeed sorry. I cannot inspect your throat."

I am summarily dismissed into the corridor outside, where I have to suck a throat-numbing sweetie for twenty minutes. Meanwhile, Mr Ghandi continues with his allocation of patients, no doubt ramming his wooden spoon gleefully down some other poor sod's oral cavity.

Eventually, with an utterly frozen throat and temporarily devoid of the ability to speak at all, I am ushered back into the consulting room by a stern-faced nurse.

"Now, let's see what we can do," smiles a benign Mr Ghandi as he unwraps a fresh wooden spoon and switches on the light in his head-gear. "Open widely, please..."

Once again, I comply readily. In goes the spoon and I feel not a thing. For a fleeting moment, I think all those nagging questions about my larynx are about to be answered, as Mr Ghandi leans tentatively towards my open mouth.

But my larynx - numbed or not - is having none of it. With rocket-like speed, the wooden spoon flies out from the dark depths of my throat, smacks Mr Ghandi's head-gear square-on and extinguishes his little light with a "pop".

... and extinguishes his little light with a "pop".

"Oh, my goodness me," is the only professional observation of my oral plight that afternoon, and I am told that I shall have to be admitted to Seacroft Hospital in Leeds for further investigation.

So now, I am *really* worried.

For the following month or two at school, I continue to give out pathetic little squeaks, and children continue to ignore me. Savage thoughts about the effects of Woodbine smoke on the human voice-box haunt my waking [and sleeping] moments. By the time I am admitted to Seacroft Hospital, I am convinced that my end is nigh.

Well, to cut a long story down a bit, I am forced into my pyjamas and told to lie down in a hospital ward for a day or two. Eventually, I am placed onto a trolley and wheeled down long, neon-lit corridors to meet an anaesthetist. He cheerfully informs me that what he is about to inject into my veins is better than five pints of Hammond's Bitter - any day of the week - and he brandishes a large syringe and needle before my very eyes.

I pass into oblivion for a period of about two hours or so...

When the mists of unconsciousness finally begin to swirl away and I start to drift back into the land of the living, the smiling face of Mr Ghandi is immediately above me.

Complete with head-gear light, he beams a smile of complete satisfaction down in my direction.

"It is alright, Mr Butler. You had several polyps on your vocal-chords, caused by straining and shouting. I have taken them away. You will be fine in a week or two."

I am ecstatic. Overjoyed to think that my larynx is once

again in fine fettle, I attempt to express my immense gratitude to Mr Ghandi, the Saviour of my Voice-Box, but all I can manage to come up with is a pathetic whimper. From the back of my battered larynx, I gurgle my words of sincere thanks.

A brief period of enforced withdrawal from work follows, during which time I say very little and am forced to wear a namby-pamby silk scarf to protect my vocal chords from the ravages of the Shoddy Town weather. Eventually, restored to full working order, I am overjoyed to return to school.

I strut the corridors and the playground once more, chancing my larynx with a shout now and again to transcend the general scholastic hubbub. As time passes, my personal klaxon returns to former decibel-levels and, for a while at least, I am overcome with gratitude to the Almighty [and to Mr Ghandi] for the gift of a voice.

But, as in most such cases, you soon forget, don't you?

It wasn't long before I was taking my powerful sonic boom for granted once again, abusing my God-given gift on a daily basis. The thoughts of what might have been were conveniently shelved away in the dark recesses of my brain-box, long forgotten and deeply buried on purpose.

But the whole experience was never *entirely* erased from my conscience.

For years afterwards, sometimes furtively sneaking along empty, silent, post-four o'clock corridors, I would gleefully prance up and down, rejoicing at the restoration of my sonic boom. A cheeky grin would light up my teacher's stern glower as I prepared for a bit of adolescent fun.

Checking carefully over my shoulder the length of the long tiled corridor to ensure that nobody was about, I'd call out, just for the sheer hell of it:

"See! HALSTEAD! Sit DOWN lad, afore Ah knock thi DOWN!"

***

DO IT  YOURSELF

I've always been one for having a go at doing things for myself. My enthusiasm for Do-It-Yourself must have been fuelled at a very early age by my Dad - who was *also* one for having a go himself...

I remember distinctly one summer's evening when I was about four years old watching my waistcoated Dad, foundryman's trilby at a jaunty angle, painting a window at the front of our house. He'd returned home after an eight-hour stint in the foundry, gulped down his tea and shot out to our garden shed. Emerging two or three minutes later with a one-inch brush, a tin of turps and a pot of paint, he'd dashed round to the front of the house to begin his evening's DIY.

The odour of that deep green paint drifts back to me across the years, and I can smell again the oily fumes from a black and white ICI tin, labelled "Buckingham Green". My junior nose is but two inches from the tin and I clutch a paint-brush from my paint-box in my sweaty little palm. I am keen to give a hand, brush poised to dip in to the thick, green liquid.

"No, Freddie. That paint's not for little boys. Little boys 'ave to use varnish - and a proper varnish brush."

For a foundryman, my Dad seemed to know a great deal about painting and decorating, but I accept his advice as he sets me up to "varnish" our front gate.

Out of the shed, he fetches an empty ICI tin and a clean one-inch paint brush. Handing me the brush and issuing a precise instruction to wait for him by the front gate, he informs me that he is going to get my paint ready for application - by me.

With infant exuberance, brush in hand, I dash to the front gate to await my pot of "special" varnish. Dad, meanwhile, sprints into the back-kitchen, fills the empty tin with water and nips out of our front door to meet me "on the job".

"Now *this*," he says indicating the tin of water, "*this* is special Boy's Front-Gate Varnish, and y'ave to be reight careful with it. Y'aven't ter get it on yer clothes, else Johnny Goblin'll 'ave yer tonight when yer go ter bed."

Wide-eyed, with the spectre of the Dreaded Dwarf JG hanging above my head, I am the very model of a careful painter as I dip in my brush and "paint" our front gate. For a while, the brushed-on water gleams and glistens with a varnish-shine in the evening sunshine. I carefully and conscientiously paint it onto the gate, spilling not a drop, and I am the picture of contentment. A DIY painter, just like my Dad.

As I complete a full coat of Boy's Front-Gate Varnish at the end of the job, I look back to cast an appreciative four-year old eye on my work. But what's this? The glistening, glossy shine at the other end has disappeared, leaving a dull and peeling coat of faded green. The gate looks remarkably the same as when I'd kicked off the job.

"Where has my coat of special varnish gone," I demand and I proceed to coat the gate all over again. Such activity keeps me busy until bed-time and well out of Dad's way as he proceeds, unhindered, with *his* painting job...

So my Do-It-Yourself enthusiasm was fired up at a very

early age, and as I grew up, my Dad encouraged me to undertake other, more ambitious projects of a fairly wide variety. By the time I was fourteen, I'd have a go at most things with some enthusiasm, given a bit of encouragement. Except for that time when I was called upon to do some butchering...

As Foundry Manager at P.& C. Garnett's, Textile Machine Makers, Cleckheaton, one of my Dad's responsibilities was the ordering and maintenance of a wholesome supply of "scrap" metal. This scrap metal was recycled, after melting it down in the furnace, for use in casting the huge rollers for the textile machines of the area - rag-grinding machines which were the very life-blood of our Shoddy Towns' industrial activity.

Now, as it happened, Dad bought all the scrap metal for Garnett's from a local dealer called Freddie Hardcastle whose yard was at Gomersal, underneath a railway arch just off the main Bradford Road. Narrow-faced, toothless, bachelor Freddie had a pronounced limp and a battered old brown trilby. He rarely removed his headgear, even when he was spending an hour or two of an evening at our house, chatting to us all about his regular flights abroad and his visits to "t'farm".

"T'farm" was Freddie's sister's small-holding at Masham in North Yorkshire, and his regular visits there often resulted in excellent farming produce arriving at his Gomersal yard for dispersal amongst his customers - a little 'thank you' for the privilege of their business. In the Butler household, we received regular supplies of potatoes by the sack-load, turnips by the boxful and cabbages by the barrow-load. Our cellar at Huddersfield Road would be brim-full of excellent North Yorkshire consumables all year round, so we growing lads were never short of essential vitamins. And Freddie Hardcastle was over the moon as he continued to receive plenty of scrap-metal orders via my Dad.

And then, one February Friday evening, quite unexpectedly, Freddie arrives at our house, not with the usual sack of 'taties' or boxful of 'tunnups', but with a freshly-killed chicken. Its recently-wrung neck swung in rhythm with Freddie's limp as he mounted our back-step and slung it casually onto our kitchen table. I remember its head swinging lifelessly off the end of the table and the deep-brown of its wings as they flapped open across that night's edition of the 'Telegraph and Argus'.

"'Ere y'are," he announced to my Mum in his usual, matter-of-fact way. "Summat fer t'Sunday dinner. It'll need dressin', though. Tha can get t'lads ter do it fo' thi..."

In my wide-eyed, adolescent configuration of things I was baffled.

I'd never before seen a dead chicken at such close quarters and when I heard the word "dressing", I pictured the said chicken in a nice floral skirt and a spring bonnet, prior to its entry into the Sunday morning oven. I wondered how such an animal, dressed like that, would end up like the crisply-roasted, golden-brown Sunday dinner my Mum usually served up.

It wasn't long before I discovered the answer to my many puzzling questions.

Shortly after Freddie's departure into the dark Friday night, my Dad lifts the dead chicken off the kitchen table and gingerly transports it down the cellar steps at arm's length. He is clearly unhappy at the close proximity of dead meat and he returns, white-faced, some minutes later. Gesturing to brother Robin and myself, he takes us quietly on one side.

With an air of confidentiality, he delivers an F.A. Butler [Senior] pronouncement: "Nahthen, this 'ere chicken'll need seein' to, before yer mother can cook it," he says, in his Foundry Manager voice. "So that's *your* job tomorrer mornin', boys. Pluck it and clean it... Right?"

We nod obediently as the truth of the matter begins to dawn.

Our Saturday morning was to be spent yanking the feathers off the dead carcass to reveal the white flesh beneath. Further to that, we were to get the chicken into its "oven-ready" state by removing parts of the legs and the contents of its insides! A spot of DIY butchering activity for our out-of-school, week-end activity.

I spend the night in fitful sleep, images of angry hens pecking at my fingers and leaping at me as I approach one of their number with intent to pluck. At regular intervals, I am yanked from slumber by leaping apparitions of smiling chickens in their Sunday-best dresses climbing into ovens. By dawn's early light, I am a shivering wreck.

At ten o'clock the following morning, the Butler Brothers are down in the dark depths of the cellar, ashen-faced and trembling. We're armed with kitchen knives, a pair of scissors and a rusty old chopper, ready to carry out our parental instructions before my Dad arrives home from his Saturday morning's earnest travail at P.&C. Garnett's.

Our Robin looks at me for instruction. He is five years my junior but he has already worked out what the first butchering activity of the morning will involve. The tears of disgust well up in his eyes and his stomach is already rumbling at the prospect of removing the dead bird's thinking apparatus.

Taking senior partner responsibility, I brandish our not-so-sharp axe.

"We've ter tek its 'eead off," I whisper hiding my fear in the bravado of Shoddy Town Speak. "Tha'll 'a' ter 'od it still wol Ah tek a swipe at it."

"Ah dadn't," says Our Robin. "Ah's'll bi sick. Ah'm gippin' already." And he dashes over to the dirty old pot sink in the corner...

Our morning's toil down the cellar begins in earnest about ten minutes later, after we have parted company with most of our half-digested cornflakes and scrambled egg breakfast. We spend the next couple of hours filling a carrier-bag with feathers which we have painstakingly yanked out of the carcass to reveal the pale, white flesh beneath.

We have already decapitated the bird and discarded its head in another carrier-bag. Also, with bare hands and with eyes tightly closed, we have reached inside the carcass and pulled out a variety of internal contents. I recall sneaking a glimpse at one handful and noticing that our chicken's entrails were multi-coloured, with greens and blues and yellows - colours I had not associated with the internal organs of any living thing.

Eventually, our carrier-bags are fairly brimming with offal as we lower them into the dustbin. Our final task is to stick a hose-pipe into the now-empty chicken, and wash away the slimy, bloody mess of its interior down the cellar-sink...

A few minutes later, whistling cheerily, Dad arrives home from his morning's foundry toil.

After hanging up his trilby and taking off his Foundry Manager's jacket, F.A. Butler [Senior] finds his two off-spring upstairs on their beds, ashen-faced and groaning profusely. They are clutching their stomachs and writhing in nauseous agony as a result of their DIY butchering activities.

"Who's off ter t'Fryin' Pan for t'fish an' chips, then, " asks Dad cheerfully.

Robin and I leap from our beds in a desperate sprint to be first into the toilet...

The following dinner time, the result of our Saturday morning DIY activities is extracted from the Sunday morning oven. Steaming appetisingly, with a crisp, golden skin and surrounded by roast potatoes, our Sunday dinner arrives at the table.

"Nahthen," enthuses my Dad, brandishing the carving-knife. "Who wants a leg?"

Robin and I leap from our seats in unison and sprint upstairs for the toilet...

After that episode, and realising his sons' lack of enthusiasm for carrying out unpleasant tasks in the face of constitutional danger, Dad was less inclined to direct our DIY activities, particularly in the field of butchery. But eventually, when the nausea had subsided and the memory of that cellar-activity had faded away, I began to use my own initiative and to undertake DIY projects of a more personal kind...

In the days long before the portable transistor radio and the audio sound systems of the modern era, I vividly recall being allowed to have a floor standing, all-electric 'radio-gram' in my bedroom, next to my bed. This state-of-the-art piece of equipment had a record-player in the top section and lower down, it contained a wireless!

So, in the late 1950's, after completing hours of ghastly BGS homework, I'd creep towards my little wooden bed. Yawning profusely, I'd switch on my wireless and rotate the dark-brown tuning knob. Staring wide-eyed at the pointer on the dimly-lit dial as it crept past "Light", "Home" and "Hilversum", I'd slow the twiddling of the knob right down at the approach of 208 on the medium wave-band.

With one ear close to the speaker, I'd listen intently for the strains of rock n' roll. But the chances were I'd hear an advertisement for Horace Batchelor and his plan for winning the pools from his base at Keynsham, Bristol. If that was the case, then I was on the right station and I could look forward to the strains of Jack Jackson and his Decca Record Show, or Kent Walton and the Capitol Label Show on Radio Luxembourg.

An hour or so of Connie Francis, Eddie Cochrane, Fats Domino and Duane Eddy [amongst many others] would see me ready for a peaceful night's slumber.

And then, one Christmas holiday in 1960, a DIY idea came to me which might possibly repair my family reputation after those disastrous events of 1959. It was a cunning plan to curry favour with my Mum who had only just come round to accepting the fact that I was a regular smoker. I felt sure that it would meet with parental approval and it hinged on the fact that my Mum was one of those 1950's house-wives whose sole aim in life was to cater for the three "men" in our family.

So that she could enjoy the delights of day-time wireless whilst she was about her household chores, I decided that I would rig up an extension speaker between the radio-gram beside my bed to our kitchen. This would mean that Mum could switch on the set next to my bed, tune in and enjoy the delights of all-day wireless downstairs. "Housewives' Choice" and "Woman's Hour" - at the flick of a switch. Such a project was bound to get me back into the parental Good Books.

Now, for the hobby section of my Duke of Edinburgh's Award Bronze level in the BGS Combined Cadet Force, I'd been studying "Electricity" so I knew all about the use of wires and switches, didn't I? Perhaps I could wire up a simple extension speaker from an old defunct wireless which had been lying about down our cellar. I could then place it on a shelf above the kitchen-sink where, in my perception of things, my Mum spent most of her working day.

The project got off to a flying start. One afternoon, I caught the 18A Heavy Woollen District Transport Omnibus down to Heckmondwike and bought far too much two-core cable from R.B.Stead's Ironmongers Shop. After tea that night, I set about taking the back off the radio-gram to access the speaker connections. I wound the bared ends of the two wires round the speaker's terminals, and replaced the back on the radio-gram. So now, I have a coil of speaker wire which I tuck away on the floor, out of sight behind the apparatus.

As I inspect the first phase of my project, I cannot help but shrug my shoulders in a resigned fashion. The length of wire on the floor appeared to be long enough to connect our Huddersfield Road house to Birkenshaw Fire Station. However, Stage One of the Curry-Favour-With-Mum Project has now been completed fairly successfully.

I'm about ready for Stage Two: to trail the wire out of my bedroom window, across the living-room bay-window roof, down the house-side and into the kitchen via the small top-opening window. The following afternoon, conditions are ideal.

The weather is fine, my Dad's step-ladders are in our garage and Mum is attending a Townswomen's Guild meeting in Liversedge. So off we go!

After gingerly clambering across the roof of the bay-window, fearing any second the creak of collapsing rafters, I lean out to grab a drain-pipe for support. With one precarious toe-hold on the drain-pipe, I stretch out over the edge of the roof-bay to feed the 300 yards of extension wire through the small kitchen window. As the length of cable flops onto the floor inside the kitchen, the hazardous part of Stage Two is over. A couple of snips with Dad's pliers later, and some neat trimming of wire with a pair of kitchen scissors, and the extension speaker is wired up and ready to go. Stage Two of the project is done and dusted.

Stage Three begins with my Mum's return home at 4.00pm.

Her entrance through the back-door is heralded by the strains of afternoon music from the shelf above the kitchen sink. She is somewhat overwhelmed by the technological advances made during her short absence. After absorbing my technical explanations as to the improvements to our sound-system, however, she is overjoyed.

Mission accomplished, thanks to BGS CCF, the Duke of Edinburgh's Award Scheme and a bit of initiative on the part of Yours Truly. Mum's favour has been suitably curried.

That evening, I feel appropriately smug as I explain my DIY home improvements to my Dad. "Well, that's a bogger," he marvels in his Nottinghamshire twang, and Number One son is back in the Good Books...

Three weeks later, my Mum ventures a comment [in Scottish] about the improved sound system: "Ev'ry time the phone rings or somebody comes tae oor door," she complains, "I have tae gang upstairs tae switch aff the wireless. Ah dinnae think it's sich a guid idea, efter a', Freddie. Ah'm fair tired oot, runnin' up and doon."

By now, my own self-confidence in the DIY field has grown to over-blown proportions.

"Fear not, Mother," I state confidently. "I shall rectify this slight hitch immediately." And I go upstairs to my bedroom to ponder the problem with particular reference to my D of E Award Electricity course. A brief study of my pencil notes reveals the facts I need. A switch to a power supply, I discover, can be installed by breaking the live [red] wire at a suitable point in the circuit and by fitting a one-way switch.

Brimming with DIY enthusiasm, I announce this fact to my

Mum. The following day, I shall catch the 18A to Heckmondwike again and purchase the necessary equipment from R.B.Stead and Son. I might even try for a refund on the 250 yards or so of spare speaker-wire that I happen to have left over. The overall cost will be met from my own pocket-money, and further favour will have been curried, I think craftily to myself.

Sure enough, the following afternoon finds me once more on my knees behind the radio-gram in my bedroom.

To my left, on the floor beside me, is a small, round metal switch, its chrome housing glinting in the rays from the ceiling light. To my right is the detached plug from the radio-gram. In front of me is the severed live-wire of the power supply to the apparatus.

All I have to do now is connect the two switch wires to the power supply with the new wire I have purchased, lead said wire via the same route as previous to the kitchen, and connect the switch. And hey presto! The radio-gram can be switched on/off from the comfort of the kitchen-sink...

A few hours later, I am driving home the final screw in the bright chrome switch, fixing it to the shelf above the sink. "Nar mi Mother can turn t'radio-gram on or off baht even brekkin' off fro' weshin' t'pots," I murmur to myself out loud in Shoddy Town Speak, so confident am I about the success of my project.

A quick flick of the switch assures me that the installation process is complete. With the radio-gram switched "on" upstairs, it is now possible to break the circuit in the power wire to it without leaving the confines of the kitchen-sink.

I proudly demonstrate the technique to my wide-eyed Mum. With one hand and a nonchalant flick of the fore-finger, I operate the little chrome switch.

"Now you hear it," I brag - and as I flick the switch off - "Now you don't..." My Mum is again suitably impressed and yet more favour has been curried.

A few days later, just before I am due to return to BGS after the Spring half-term holiday, a wet Monday afternoon finds me desperately trying to catch up on the homework we'd been set for the holiday period. I pore over my maths text book at our living-room table. My Mum is in the kitchen, besieged by piles of damp washing.

Unable to hang any of it out to dry, she is behind on the wash-day schedule, so our stainless-steel kitchen sink is full to the brim with water and a pile of my shirts. Mum is arduously scrubbing a particularly grubby collar, but her task is eased somewhat by the pleasant strains of "Variety Bandbox" from the speaker above her on the shelf.

The telephone rings in the hall. Mum decides to answer it, but first, she will avail herself of the conveniently installed remote switching system to turn off her afternoon music.

Right hand resting on the rim of the sink, she reaches up with the other hand to switch off the radio-gram, as permitted by the installation of the said system, devised by Yours Truly. With *wet* hands touching a live metal switch and an equally *wet* hand on the *wet* metal sink, she completes the electrical circuit with the rest of her body.

From our living-room , I hear a loud Scottish yelp of painful anguish "Oh, Michty me! Help me, Freddie!"

Sensing the urgency of the situation by her tone, I race into the kitchen.

Mum is transfixed over by the sink. One hand remains electrically glued to the metal switch on the shelf above her and there is a buzzing, sizzling sound as waves of electricity course through her entire body. Her hair leaps skywards from her scalp and maintains a vertical orientation, despite the body-wracking tremors which convulse her substantial frame.

"*Hell's buckets,*" says my Inner Shoddy Town Voice. "*She's throwin' a fit.*"

"Turn the bloody thing aff, ye' daft gowk," she yells in Scottish over her quivering shoulder as the sizzling sound increases.

I race over to the sink, unsure of what to do. Should I race upstairs and switch off the radio-gram? Or should I dash down into the cellar and pull out the fuse? The Duke of Edinburgh's Award Scheme Electricity course notes had not been clear on such procedures. In the meantime, Mum is fairly sizzling and buzzing at the sink next to me.

While I am still ponderously considering my response to her current plight, my Shoddy Town Inner Voice comes to the rescue: "*Gerr od on 'er 'and an' pull it off o' t'switch, yer silly sod!*"

Suitably admonished and without touching any of the nearby metal, I wrench my Mum's hand away from the chromed steel switch of the remote switching system. Mother collapses in a jelly-like heap on the floor. She looks up at me with a glazed expression: "Oh, Michty me! Ah cannae see straight an' there's som'b'dy on the 'phone..."

By the time I reach the telephone, it has stopped ringing. By the time my Dad returns home from the foundry that evening, the remote switching system has been dismantled, disarmed and discontinued...

With an experience such as that under my adolescent belt, you'd have thought that I'd have given Do-It-Yourself projects an extremely wide berth in the future. After all, as a result of assuming I knew all about the complexities of electrical circuits, I'd just about electrocuted my own mother. A little knowledge is a dangerous thing.

But as in the field of amateur dramatics, so in that of DIY - there is perhaps something of the lemming inherent in practitioners of both. So whenever a home repair or improvement idea is mooted, my first reaction was [and still is]: "Can I tackle this job myself?" My Shoddy Town Inner Voice, however, often has other ideas: "*Dooan't be ser daft, lad. Yond job's ter much fer thee. Get thisen a reight bloke ter do it fo' thi.*"

Nevertheless, one Spring morning in 1976 some 16 years after the Maternal Electrocution Incident, I find myself looking skywards at the roof of our Batley semi-detached house. Married now, with mortgage responsibilities, I stand dejectedly on the pavement and contemplate the ravaging effects of a severe winter on our chimney-pot. In its exposed location at the top of Soothill, our current dwelling has been exposed to the blast of the winter winds and gales which howl up the valley from the calmer climes of Bradford Road down below.

Shielding my eyes from the bright morning sun, I note that

winter has indeed taken its destructive toll. Several fallen pieces of cement-pointing have come to rest half-way down the slope of the roof. The gutters are beginning to sag under the weight of dross that has blown off the tiles, and some of the lead flashing round the chimney pot has begun to curl and lift away from its original position.

The roof over our heads is in dire need of urgent attention.

Now, as recounted elsewhere in these Shoddy Town Tales, I'd served a sort of semi-apprenticeship in the building trade during my student days at John Crosslands, Builders, Cleckheaton. I knew all about laying bricks, spreading concrete and mixing "compo", didn't I? In that respect, Life had been a hard task-master but an excellent teacher.

I'd learned about digging out "footings" from many of the navvying gang-members it had been my privilege to work alongside. I'd picked up one or two bricklaying skills from men like one-toothed, flat-capped Percy Barber who'd explained, in great detail, how I might create a brick/stone arch. But most important of all, I'd learned about mixing mortar and concrete at the ratio of "four to one" from Stuart Bentley who supervised my efforts as a first-time brickie's labourer on a job down Forge Lane in Liversedge.

I can utilise all those skills and bring them to bear on my present task, can't I? As I survey my Batley chimney-pot, stroking my chin thoughtfully and assessing the skills required for the job in hand, my mind drifts back to my very first efforts at mixing sand and cement for a building job such as this...

For most of July and August, 1963, I'd been stationed at Burnley's Gomersal mill as an employee of the

Crossland's Building Team, where my youthful student energy and exuberance had been channelled into mixing concrete and laying floors. Quite substantial quantities of mixed concrete were required for the various repair jobs at the mill, so a hefty piece of machinery was in use to provide the necessary quantities in bulk. It was a huge, ten feet tall, diesel-engined concrete mixer with a great steel hopper at the front. Up the side of the mixer ran a steel gantry and at the top, there was a pulley-wheel, round which ran a chain. This, in turn, was attached to the back of the afore-mentioned hopper.

Towering above the banking on which it stood at the top side of the mill yard, the whole affair stood silent sentinel overlooking Firthcliffe, Cleckheaton and the whole of the Spen Valley. It was a vista to take your Shoddy Town breath away, but, we were oblivious to such panoramic views. Our labourers' task did not allow for any sight-seeing. We were kept far too busy regularly filling the hopper of this mechanical giant with the ingredients for concrete, starting up the hefty diesel engine and preparing to tip the loaded hopper into the gaping mouth of the huge, revolving mixer drum.

We'd been given a special recipe for the mixing of the said concrete. This comprised four barrow-loads of gravel, two barrow loads of river sand and one bag of cement - known in the trade as "six ter one".

Now, arduous as it was, I quite enjoyed this particular job.

I would whistle cheerfully as I shovelled sand and gravel into my wheelbarrow and trundled my loads off to tip them into the waiting mouth of the hopper, which, at this time, was at ground level. The final addition of a bag of cement from the store-hut near the foreman's cabin was all that was now required to complete the "six ter one" mix, and the fun part of the job began.

A hefty turn on the cranking-handle, and the diesel engine would splutter into black, smoky life. A deft pull on a lever near the base of the afore-mentioned gantry, and the fully-laden hopper began its agonisingly slow upward journey towards the mouth of the waiting, revolving mixer-drum.

The pulley-wheel creaked and groaned under the strain of its hefty load, but finally the hopper arrived at its destination. As the mix of sand, gravel and cement fell into the drum, all you had to do to ensure a creamy-rich concrete mixture was to nip up the side of the gantry, hose-pipe in hand. A carefully judged quantity of water could then be introduced into the mix to ensure the correct consistency.

When all was ready, the machinery could be activated to tip the contents of the drum into the waiting bucket of a dumper truck, which would be positioned in readiness. Now for the delivery stage of the mix, to the waiting labourers, leaning on their shovels, round the other side of the complex.

For me, this represented another fun-filled facet of the job. Yours Truly, driving the dumper-truck round the tar-mac perimeter of Burnley's mill at a break-neck speed of fifteen miles per hour - when I hadn't even passed my driving test! Upon arrival at the job-site, I scream to a halt and yank the tipper handle beside my right knee. The bucket leaps forward, its contents splatter out onto the hard-core and wire-mesh floor and the waiting labourers set to with their shovels and boards to flatten my mix to a mirror-finish.

Meanwhile, back I go to have yet more fun on the concrete-mixer...

So for several weeks now, I'd been having the time of my life as I ferried more and more of the thick, grey concrete-mix around the mill-site. But then, in the form of portly Joe Dickinson, the site foreman, a heavy cloud dampened my student's spirit of fun and enjoyment

Joe sidled up to me one evening towards the end of our working day, just as I was hosing down the dumper-truck's bucket - known technically as "weshin' aht".

Shifting his flat cap to the back of his head, Joe took me on one side. "Nahthen, young 'un," he says confidentially. "Tha'll be workin' wi Stuart Bentley an' young Jagger tomorn."

He named two of the skilled young bricklayers whom I'd met earlier in the summer but with whom I'd never worked.

"Tha'll be labourin' for 'em at number 69 Forge Lane, start 8 o'clock. Garage job at an 'ouse. Tha'll be reight for a few cups o' teea from t'woman 'at lives theer, if tha plays thi cards reight."

So that was it. No more loading up the hopper and operating the diesel-engined hoist. No more driving round the mill perimeter like a Lord of the Road in my big dumper-truck. And no more joyful dinner-time banter in the Crossland's cabin with George Wilkinson, Big Ned, Peter Leary and Bert Lockwood. My education at the University of Life would no doubt suffer as a result.

All things considered, I left Burnley's mill shortly afterwards, downcast and disappointed. I made my glum way to the bus-stop on the road outside and listened carefully to my Inner Voice. Seeing as we weren't at our London college training to be a teacher, it chose to address me in Shoddy Town Speak:

"*Tha'll be reight,*" it whispered comfortingly. "*Stuart an' young Jagger are abaht t'same age as thee, so tha can 'ave a bit on a laugh wi' 'em, can't ta?*"

And it continued to comfort me all the way home.

"*Tha'll be able to walk ter thi work an' it weean't cost as much i' bus-fares. <u>An'</u> tha'll gerrooam sooiner fer thi teea, owd lad...*"

By the time I alighted the Heavy Woollen District Transport Company omnibus at the Bar House, my Inner Voice had convinced me that leaving behind those enjoyable activities at Burnley's mill wasn't altogether such a bad thing. I began to look forward to my next day at work as a labourer for two skilled men.

The next bright summer morning finds me whistling my way along the field footpath opposite our Huddersfield Road house and down the snicket next to the old tin chapel on Liversedge Hall Lane. Minutes later, I arrive at number 69 Forge Lane, just off Cornmill Lane, to be greeted by the young Stuart Bentley who is in charge. Tall, dark-haired Stuart stands in the driveway of the house peering up and down the lane. He is a quietly spoken young man, unassuming in his role as "gaffer" on this particular job. At the moment, he seems a little agitated.

"Jagger 'an't peeked yet," he mutters to me, in obvious exasperation at the missing half of his bricklaying team.

"We've ter finish buildin' this 'ere garage in a couple o' days, an' the bugger's late already. Tha'd better get a mixin' on, owd cock - for when we start."

He indicates a small cement mixer at the back of the house alongside some stacks of bricks, a pile of building sand and several bags of cement. "We's'll kick off as sooin as Jagger peeaks."

"Reight, Stuart," says I, anxious to please my new Gaffer. Displaying my technical knowledge as to the complexities of cement-mixing, I ask: "'Ow dusta want it?"

Stuart is well impressed. I can almost hear him thinking to himself: "For a student, this lad knows a thing or two abaht t'buildin' trade."

Out loud, he instructs me: "Fower ter one, Freddie owd lad. Fo' t'bricklayin', it's allus fower ter one."

I shoot off to the mixer, brimming with a young labourer's enthusiasm.

Now, up to this point in my building career, I'd been mixing concrete for vast mill floors up at Burnley's Mill, so all quantities were meticulously measured out in barrowloads, as previously recounted. The addition of a final bag of cement to the hopper completed the mix. Here at Forge Lane, I am meeting the "compo" needs of two bricklayers, so a mixture of "fower ter one" indicated - to those in the know - four *shovelfuls* of sand with one *shovelful* of cement to be added.

But I am new to the bricklaying task, and am still operating in concrete-flooring mode. I set to with a fiery enthusiasm.

Starting the little diesel mixer was easy enough and soon, I have flung four shovelfuls of sand into the revolving drum. All that remains now is the addition of the cement and the water to provide a creamy rich mixture of "compo" for my bricklaying chums.

Just as I have been doing at Burnley's Mill, I empty the entire contents of a bag of cement into the mouth of the mixer. Water is added - rather a lot, I thought at the time - and soon I have positioned my wheelbarrow under the mixer and tipped out the ready-mixed load. A grey mass of stodgy clay lands with a thud in my barrow and I trundle off down the drive to make my delivery.

Arriving at the front gate, I find that the tardy Jagger has at last arrived. A swarthy, stocky lad in his late teens, he is not much older than his labourer, whom he greets with a cursory nod.

"Tha'r a bit keen aren't ta," he mutters. "Gerrin' a mixin' on afore we've 'ad t'chance fer a pot o' teea."

I'm about to explain that, prior to his late arrival, the Gaffer on this job had already instructed me to get started, when I notice Stuart peering enquiringly [in Gaffer-style] at the contents of my barrow. After a couple of strolls round the front end and several critical sniffs, he addresses me without taking his eye off the pudding-like clod in my barrow.

"What's tha call this, then? What's ta done 'ere, Fred, owd cocker?" And he sticks a sturdy, inspectorial finger into the mixture.

"Ah've getten thee a mixin', Stuart," I announce with pride, in building-site Shoddy Town Speak. "Like tha telled mi - 'fower ter one'."

"Nivver," retorts the astonished Stuart. "It's like a lump o' mi mother's suet. That's nivver fower ter one i' this wide world. Oh, Jagger," he calls. "Bring thi trowel over 'ere a minit."

Jagger joins the inquest and attempts to slide his bricklayer's trowel into my rapidly solidifying dough. He winces in agony and exclaims: "By gow, it's near broken mi f...... wrist. If that's fower ter one, my arse is pink..."

At this stage, I am beginning to grow uneasy. These lads have been in the building trade since leaving school at fifteen, while I'd chosen to continue my lily-white-handed, academic studies at Batley Grammar School. They know all there is to know about laying bricks and mixing 'compo', so if they say that my mix is not up to scratch, then there must be something amiss with it.

I continue to state my case with lame conviction: "Ah tell thi, it's fower ter one! Fower shovels o' sand and one bag o' cement. If tha dun't believe mi, tha can see t'empty bag over yonder." I jerk an indicative thumb over my shoulder towards the mixer.

A knowing smile lights up Stuart's face. "A *bag* o' cement? An 'ole *bag*? Am Ah 'earin' thi reight, Fred? Did ta say tha'd purr an 'ole *bag* in t'mixer wi' fower shovels o' sand?"

"Aye, reight enough," I nod uneasily, sensing that something is wrong. "Fower ter one, like tha said, Stuart."

"Well, Ah'll tell thi summat nar," chuckles Stuart. "When they ask mi abaht this job, Ahs'll tell 'em: Fred Butler's worked on this garage - *an' it's built ter last!*"

He and Jagger chuckle and guffaw at my incredulity as they

"... an' it's built ter last!"

turn away. They pick up their tackle-bags and amble off in the morning sunshine towards the pile of bricks and that garage-job of forty years ago …

Back in the here-and-now, I smile to myself at the recollection, but the moment soon passes and it's time to tackle my current DIY project: re-pointing our chimney-stack.

A few minutes later, my ladder is leaning up against the house and I am at its foot. In my right hand, I clutch a bucket containing an assortment of tools required for the current job. More importantly, however, another large bucket at the foot of the ladder contains a quantity of 'compo' for the pointing job in hand. This mixture has been correctly made - four shovelfuls of sand and one *shovelful* of cement.

Whistling a happy tune, I am soon at the top of my ladder. My buckets of materials required for the job are resting on the concrete-tiles, and I am clambering, rather awkwardly, onto the slope of the roof. I prepare to make my way up towards the winter-ravaged chimney-stack.

From ground-level, this had seemed to be a fairly straight-forward task. I'd been high up on scaffolding when I'd served my labourer's apprenticeship at Crossland's, so height was not a worry. But walking up the considerable slope of a house-roof with nothing to hold on to for support was of some major concern, I can tell you!

About an hour later, I have managed to crawl gingerly on all fours up and down the roof several times, ferrying my tackle for the job to and from the gutter's edge up to the chimney stack. Trembling with anxiety and fear, I daredn't turn about to crawl down the slope, so all my journeys have been completed facing one way. By the time all my tackle *and* my bucket of correctly-mixed 'compo' is resting on the angle of the ridge tiles, the beads of fear-induced sweat are glistening on my brow. But I am ready to begin work.

I pause for a moment to quell my pounding heart-beat. Straddling the apex of the roof and clutching the red-tiled chimney pot beside me for safety's sake, I cast an appreciative eye across the fields at the back of our house towards the urban sprawl of the Shoddy Town beneath me.

In the morning sunshine, I can see the glint and sparkle of the Bradford Road traffic as it creeps along in the valley below. Newsome's Mill chimney towers above the terraced rows of Batley Carr. Steepling up the far side of the valley, the slopes of Mount Pleasant contain a myriad of Batley dwellings, each with its own daily Shoddy Town life unfolding. The Town Hall clock, over to my right, ticks relentlessly on, as it has done for the past century or so. For a moment, I feel good to be alive and to be a part of this vibrant Batley township with a history stretching back way beyond the roots of the shoddy trade.

Suddenly, a gentle breeze across my cheek reminds me that I am about three hundred feet above all that I survey - and then a few feet more to allow for the height of our Batley semi-detached! I renew my left-handed life-line grip on the chimney-pot, and begin my work...

A couple of hours later, I have completed the job. With a sense of relief, I begin the relay of my tackle to the guttering at the top of my ladder which peeps invitingly above the tiles - my stairway to the safety of *terra firma*.

But first, I have to complete another ferrying job on all fours, stacking my tackle at the roof-edge ready for its descent. This is particularly hairy because the first stage of the journey to the edge is a downhill trajectory.

As the road beneath me is quiet and deserted, I decide to employ the bum-slide mode of travel. Nobody is around to witness my inept slither down the slope, legs stretched out in front of me, using my backside as an effective brake. By such a method, I am able to carry my bucket and trowels at a snail's pace to the roof-edge, where I place them carefully in the gutter near the top of the ladder.

Terrified of turning over onto my knees for the return trip to the chimney-pot, I perform a reverse bum-slide back up the slope of the roof to fetch the remaining articles of equipment. Digging my heels into the flat surface of the tiles, I bend my knees and then shove my legs out straight, grinding another good layer of denim off the seat of my workman's jeans.

After an hour or so, I am ready for my own personal descent. Slithering gingerly to the edge, I lay the last of my tackle in the gutter and contemplate my *modus operandi* for leaving the roof.

The top of my ladder awaits me, peeping invitingly some nine or so inches above the edge of the roof. I sit before it, feet resting in the gutter and ponder. My Inner Voice makes a few proposals in Shoddy Town Speak: "*Nahthen lad. Tha's ter get thi booit inter t'top o' yon ladder baht 'angin' on. Tha can stick thi' leg aht over t'gutter, if tha wants. Burr Ah'll tell thi nah - tha bahna struggle - 'cos there's nowt ter grab 'od on.*"

At this point, I realise that I am well and truly stuck. In true DIY style, my ladder has been incorrectly positioned, with insufficient height above the gutter to allow me to climb on to it. It is abundantly clear that I cannot clamber over the edge of the considerable slope of the roof in order to descend.

Miserably, I crawl back up the roof to the relative safety of the chimney-pot to consider my next move.

It is beyond my DIY dignity and completely out of the question to shout for help. What would the neighbours think, say or do in order to effect my rescue? I should become a Soothill laughing stock and tales of my plight would reverberate around the Working Men's Club, the Cricket Club and the "Babes in the Wood" pub for years. So that option was definitely out.

I could consider a leap for safety onto our small front lawn, but this may result in severe injury to my kicking apparatus. As a result, I would have to forfeit my right to selection for the Wheelwright Old Boys Third XI this coming Saturday. Again, an unthinkable solution to my problem.

By now, I have begun to run out of possible courses of action. Perhaps I am doomed to spend the rest of my days up here on the roof above our Shoddy Town until the flesh drops from my aching bones. I imagine a plaque, placed on the house-wall by my grieving family, a testament to all would-be DIYers:

"R.I.P. Fred Butler. He passed on, trowel in hand and the other down the chimney-pot..."

Now, to add to my misery, an increasing number of passers-by is beginning to walk along our little cul-de-sac. They are mainly Mums and Dads on their way to collect off-spring from the school at the end of the street. They wave cheerily as they pass the time of day with the workman on the roof of Number Three. I cannot/must not let them know of my plight.

"Afternoon, Fred lad," shouts Malcolm Charlesworth - a life-long BGS buddy from Number Seven. "Doin' a bit o' pointin', are yer?"

Hastily grabbing a trowel and looking efficiently busy, I nod nonchalantly. "Well, these jobs 'ave ter be done, Malcolm, owd lad." With an empty trowel, I pretend to re-point the opposite side of the chimney-stack.

Minutes later, Keith Gatenby - Deputy Head and Local Councillor - passes on his way to the corner shop.

"Fred," he exclaims. "What on Earth are you doin' up there? You'll catch a chill in that wind. Don't you think you ought to come down and have a cup of tea?"

"Nay, Keith," I shout back, oozing false confidence. "Ah 'aven't time fer cups o' tea. Ah've ter finish this job afore it drops dark."

Keith shrugs a resigned shoulder and ambles off to the shop.

So now, there is but one course of action open to me: somehow, I must get my feet into the top rungs of my ladder.

Turning over onto my belly, and in full view of several young mothers who have stopped to witness the spectacle, I begin a reverse slither down the concrete tiles of the roof. The rough surface of the tiles scrapes my bared belly with an audible grating sound, and I slide down the roof at a considerable pace. My workman's jeans are yanked upwards in the opposite direction to my downward trajectory and as a result, my nether regions are subjected to excruciating compression inside my underpants. My eyes water and for a moment, I fancy that I lose consciousness.

Coming to, I dig my finger nails into the rough grey surface just in time to act as a feeble brake. My toes finally crash into the gutter and several fixing screws wrench loose, but I slither to an ungainly halt. There is a gasp from the watching group below.

I have at last arrested my downhill flight, so I pause, arms outstretched, face down, toes in the gutter, to take stock.

If I am to effect a safe descent, I need to get my feet into the top rungs of my ladder. Unable to look over my shoulder in my current face-down prone position, this will mean that I have to wave my legs out over the top six inches of my ladder and attempt to locate the top rung by feel.

Sanctimoniously, My Inner Voice warns me of the consequences: "*If tha does that, owd lad, thi knackers'll catch on t'top o' t'ladder - an' they've already tekken a bit o' stick. Tha wants ter be careful, tha knows- it'll squash 'em ter buggery.*"

But it's too late for bodily caution. The gutter into which my toes have jammed, is beginning to creak and waver under my weight. My finger nails have begun to lose their slim grip of the tiles and I anticipate another downward slide.

The watching crowd below are hushed in anticipation.

In a last desperate bid for safety, I wave my legs out over the ladder in enquiring fashion, seeking the merest toe-hold on any available rung. After what seems an age, during which my Inner Shoddy Town Voice's predictions about my nether regions are realised in full, my left toe locates something metallic. It is the side of the ladder - not the safety of a rung - but I care not a jot, such is my desperation to quit that awful roof.

I place my weight on what I take to be the rung of the ladder and slide all the way down to the floor, feet out wide, many inches from any rung whatsoever. I crash into the ground with a knee-shattering thud, and the watching crowd are well-impressed. I receive a round of applause and many hushed appreciative comments before people continue about their daily business further along the street.

Moments later, a section of guttering creaks, groans and crashes to the floor in front of me.

Dazed and bedraggled, I give it a numbed look.

"Looks like another bit o' DIY fer thi, Fred, lad," mutters my Inner Voice, confidentially. *"or tha' could gerr a reight bloke ter do it fo' thi..."*

***

THAT'S  ENTERTAINMENT

I suppose, like most teachers, I've always fancied myself as a bit of a thespian. After all, you appear before an extremely hyper-critical audience every day of your working life. If your teacher's act is going down like a lead brick, then the thirty or so members of your classroom audience will soon let you know. And that's how it was for me throughout thirty years of my Shoddy Town life...

The morning sun streams in through the large picture-windows of the comfortable Staff Room. Its rays cut through the smokey-blue atmosphere in searchlight fashion and bounce around the yellowing walls. There is a quiet hum of academic conversation punctuated by the friendly tinkle of teaspoons in coffee cups which is faintly reassuring of a life outside the confines of the school.

Easing myself into Phase One of my working day has been easy enough, but now I stretch out in my dilapidated staff-room chair and brace myself for Phase Two. The clarion call to action will come at any second.

The hand on the staff room clock clicks audibly to 9am and the harsh jangle of a bell - reminiscent of a cow urinating in a steel bucket - shatters the calm morning air. Like Pavlovian dogs, we rise from our easy chairs, grab piles of exercise-books and briefcases, and make our ways to the door.

Outside, on the red-tiled corridor, the school's new day has leapt into noisy life. Seven hundred adolescent boys and girls crash into the corridors from the play-ground. With the noisy enthusiasm of youth, they are bursting for six hours of exciting educational experiences.

So now, the acting begins. You pass along the heaving, bubbling corridor and you become larger than life - a caricature of yourself. You are about to impose your will on groups of young children at hourly intervals throughout the day [with an hour off for dinner]. For you, entry into the classroom is a dramatic daily event, charged with theatrical electricity. If you droop your shoulders, gaze dismally down at the floor and drag your tired, dejected heels towards your desk, someone in your audience of thirty will pass comment:

"Wot's up, sir? Bin on t'ale, last neet?"

Or:

"Tha looks as if thi cat's dee'd, sir."

Such observations were not, as you might think, made out of disrespect or cheekiness. Rather, they were a genuine appraisal of your current performance to date, and they indicated the perceptive qualities of observation inherent in your young audiences.

Despite any other world-shattering events from life outside the classroom, I always found that the best policy for entry onto that daily educational stage was to act my head off. For about thirty years or so, at the threshold of all my Shoddy Town classrooms, I became Sir John Gielgud, John Wayne and Steve McQueen all rolled up into one stage-struck school teacher...

Outside on the corridor, my hand fastens round the brass

knob of the classroom door. I hoist my shoulders to full height and flex my tired eyes. Adopting a false, beaming smile, I give every impression of that wide-eyed, bright-as-an-Easter-bunny look as I burst into the room. I am the epitome of energy and enthusiasm - the finest thing to hit the education market since the invention of logarithms.

"Good morning, everybody!" I boom. And to the sleep-logged dullard on the back row, yet to wake from his long night's slumber: "You too, Summerscales!"

I deliver my welcome speech with all the panache and swagger of a Shakespearean actor. "And what delights await our enquiring minds today, then, eh? An hour of mathematical mystification? Sixty minutes of geographical perambulation? Three thousand six hundred seconds of *Physical Education*?"

My class think I am an escapee from a mental institution, but most of them smile forgivingly. I note the continuing glum looks of apathy from the back row and the secretive muttering behind raised hands: " 'E must be off 'is chump."

But on this occasion, I refrain from any prolonged discussion as to my mental state. With a dramatic edge to my voice, I announce Town Crier-style: "And now, ladies and gentlemen, the register!"

My classroom charges fall into the first ritual response of their educational day: "One, sir; two, sir; three, sir..."

Head down, I complete the blue and white grid of the daily educational record before me on the desk. The column of marks unrolls on the page: / [present]; 0 [in red - absent]. And as the column gradually fills with today's vital attendance statistics, my mind drifts back to long-gone audiences of yester-year...

I'm in front of another, very different crowd now - my first ever thespian performance. I have accepted the rôle of third servant [from the left] in 'The The Servant of Two Masters', Batley Grammar School annual play, February, 1959.

My 3alpha Form Master, Mr Gill, was producing the dramatic offering, and he had persuaded me to take on a very minor part. I had three lines of fairly obscure, unimportant dialogue to be exchanged with the leading character, played by Dave Stott.

Now, 'Stotty' was a dimunitive, dark-haired Sixth Former and a live-wire of thespian activity. His enthusiasm for his rôle along with his ability to learn his lines and add to them [as he saw fit] was the envy of all we 'nobbuts' in the play.

My only entry on stage required me, as a lackey servant, to transport a dish of trifle onto the set and to exchange the said three lines with Stotty - the hero of the piece. During the action, Stotty was to irreverently dip a finger into the trifle and sample it, before delivering it for consumption to the Master of the House.

Rehearsals throughout January and February dinner-times had all gone well. I'd delivered my three short lines with a fair degree of theatrical panache, prompting favourable comments from Producer Gill. By the time we had reached the 'very-close-to-first-night' phase of events, I'd even added to my part in true 'coarse acting' style by taking a cloth on stage with me and pretending to wipe the rim of the dish clean before handing it over to the smiling Stotty.

So now, the nervous energy has stoked up to boiling point and we are approaching 7.30 pm on the opening night. An audience of proud parents, civic dignitaries and mocking BGS mates has gathered in the Graves Hall. The expectant hum of conversation subsides as the school orchestra strikes up. There's five minutes before curtain-up and there's no going back now.

Producer Gill is on obvious tenterhooks. Back-stage, he flits round the cast, nervously checking details of costume and props.

"Got your trifle, Butler?" His voice is a tremulous whisper. "Remember that it's for real now - specially prepared in the school kitchen this lunch-time."

"Oh yes, sir," I nod with an air of false confidence.

Up to now, I'd been rehearsing with an empty bowl. How was I going to manage a dish of the proper stuff? Would it be the same shape as the one used in rehearsals? Was it going to be too heavy to manage on stage? All these ridiculous questions buzzed around my brain-box as I dashed over to the props table in a corridor off-stage. There, I discovered that my scripted "trifle" was, in fact, a glass dish filled to within an inch of the top with delicious school custard.

My carry-on prop had been prepared earlier that day by School Cook, a small, rotund middle-aged lady with raven hair tied up in a bun beneath a regulation white caterer's hat. Along with her squad of Helpers, School Cook prepared an array of nourishing daily fare for consumption by we Gluttonous Grammar School boys. She had become a much-loved icon in our BGS culture and, for some reason, we'd given her the affectionate nick-name of "Blackball

Annie", but this was no criticism of her culinary abilities.

Top of our alimentary list was School Custard, a delightfully sweet, creamy, golden nectar which was always the crowning touch to any BGS school dinner. And here, before my very eyes on the props table, is a dish of that self-same culinary delight - no less appetising even though it was cold.

I pick it up as if it was my only little chick and cradle it tenderly in my arms. Carefully and cautiously, I make my way into the wings in preparation for my entry cue. I am in good time, for the curtain has only just gone up and the first scene has just nicely got under way.

I settle down in a dark corner of the wings for quite a long wait.

A few minutes on, still lovingly cradling my dish of custard, I look up into the void above me and mentally rehearse my three lines. A casual finger-end dips into the creamy yellow mixture in my bowl. Regarding the offending digit absent-mindedly, I am challenged by my Inner Voice in Shoddy Town Speak:

"Tha can't goo on ter t'stage wi' all yon custard drippin' off thi finger-end, can ta? Tha'll 'a' ter get rid."

Answering my Inner Voice challenge like a man, I gingerly lick the offending digit clean.

The taste of that sweet nectar, for which we would gladly have committed murder each week-day dinner-time, is rapturously sublime. I risk another dip and re-rehearse my lines. It is too good to be true. Twenty or so minutes before I am due on stage - and a whole dish of custard to go at!

"Stottie weean't miss a scoddy little bit 'o custard, will 'e," urges my Inner Voice. *"Goo on - 'ave another dip."*

About fifteen minutes later, my belly is full to capacity of delicious, school custard, but, alas, my bowl is empty. A couple of minutes after that, Stottie delivers my entry cue with a dramatic flourish. A split second later and I'm on stage with an empty bowl of "trifle".

The dialogue with the star of the show proceeds and I begin to experience that sinking feeling which I was to encounter repeatedly throughout the next few years of my bungling thespian career.

The inevitable cue is hurtling unstoppably towards you. You are without a vital item of stage property/the correct line of a speech/ a very important piece of costume. Short of turning to the audience and making an extremely important announcement: *"Ladies and gentlemen, would you please excuse me while I exit, stage left, to collect a vital item of stage property. Just talk amongst yourselves and pretend that you haven't seen this bit yet..."*, there's absolutely nothing you can do about it.

As feelings go, it's one of the worst in the Whole Wide World. On this first occasion in 1959 at Batley Grammar School, during "The Servant of Two Masters" Act One, Scene Two, I experienced it to the maximum.

To his credit, Stottie was magnificent. Without batting a theatrical eye-lid, he talked his way round our three-line dialogue, the topic of which should have been the quality of the [now-missing] "trifle". During his rambling effort to return to the genuine script, I am left gob-smacked and speechless. I stare at him open-mouthed, and within a few seconds, I receive my exit cue and depart the stage, none of my carefully rehearsed three lines having been delivered

In the wings, Producer Gill is purple-faced furious. Using an enforced back-stage whisper, he hisses out an almighty rollicking, and allocates me with a standard BGS punishment for all misdemeanours - a Saturday Morning Detention. I am *persona non grata* on the Graves Hall stage for the next eighteen months until this incident has blown over.

But time marches on. Stottie leaves school to continue his studies at Oxford University; Producer Gill leaves Batley for a job down south in Barnsley; and I am once more allowed to tread the BGS boards under the direction of Irving L. Theaker, newly appointed teacher of English...

So you'd think, having experienced a thespian baptism such as mine, that I'd have steered well clear of any future theatrical involvement. But perhaps there's something of the lemming inherent in we theatrical types, and this probably drives us on into the ranks of the bit players in amateur dramatics. Be that as it may, some ten years after that baptism of fire in the Graves Hall, I have developed some confidence about the daily art of coarse acting. I strut my teacher's stuff across the classroom floor, performing my "act" before quite a few Shoddy Town kids.

As part of my daily efforts to earn an honest crust, I'd become familiar with the art of pretending. Early on in my teaching career, I'd discovered that rarely is a teacher *really* angry when he berates a miscreant for misbehaviour; and that seldom is that same teacher *really* over the educational moon when he praises a commendable piece of good work.

So a prerequisite for much classroom activity of any kind was a generous allocation of "pretend".

Day in, day out, many a Shoddy Town kid was severely reprimanded in my entirely false, "I-am-about-to-lose-my-temper" voice. Similarly, many kids have returned to their classroom desks after a consultation on a current piece of written work sporting a huge beam of delight.

"An absolutely marvellous piece of English Literature, Fothergill," I'd enthuse to the scruffy member of my 4c English group who'd just presented a page of his earnest written endeavour.

"Top marks for effort, lad. Do you know, this essay richly deserves a Nobel Peace Prize, but seeing as I haven't one handy, you'll have to make do with this Extra Strong Mint..."

In 1969, at Earlsheaton School, our Head of English is the long-haired, bespectacled Geoffrey Holmes, a talented writer and producer with the then embryonic Dewsbury Arts Group. Struggling to find numbers to fill the huge cast of the "Caucasian Chalk Circle", Geoffrey invites Yours Truly to play third soldier [from the left] in the Arts Group's current production of Brecht's play.

And at that point in my Shoddy Town life, my still dormant thespian career is yanked from its erstwhile slumber.

Over the following years, I readily accept parts in many and varied plays - usually comedies - where there is ample opportunity both on stage and during rehearsals, to indulge in many a comic side-splitting moment...

Quite the funniest man it has ever been my privilege to act

alongside is Andrew Madden whose nick-name in the Arts Group was [and still is] "Archie".

Wiry and slight in appearance, balding Archie Madden is one of Life's characters who has the gift of being able to spread laughter wherever he goes. A knowing look and a glint in his twinkling eye is Archie's signal that some cleverly-conceived, comic remark is about to be made. Rarely is this humour spiteful or derogatory. It is borne of a perceptive eye for the comedy of real life situations, and its effects can reduce even the most stern-faced individual to fits of helpless laughter.

It is December, 1970 and the Dewsbury Arts Group's children's play is in full swing. Staged this year at Dewsbury Town Hall, our current offering is the famous "Treasure Island", adapted for the stage by David Wood, another of our local group's most outstanding talents. Yours Truly has landed the part of George Merry - a pirate with six or seven lines of script to be delivered in a Robert Newton-like West Country brogue.

Liberally lacing my scant lines with plenty of additional "Ooh arrs", and skilfully directed by producer Russell Whiteley, I am enjoying the experience of chasing round the stage in waistcoat, breeches and pirate bandana. The pirate gang's exits and entrances along the aisles of the auditorium are a splendid feature of the production, encouraging our child-audience "to feel involved".

Through the vast auditorium of the magnificent Victorian Town Hall, packed tight with over-excited, charged-up, full-of-pop-n'-crisps, Shoddy Town Littl'uns, our pirate gang makes its evil way off the stage in search of buried treasure. Led by Long John [David Wood] Silver with his leg strapped up behind him out of sight under his green pirate's coat, we leer nastily at the kids in the surrounding seats as we leave down the centre aisle. We are treating them to the thrill of theatrical "fear" whilst we "ooh arr" our way towards the great double doors at the back.

As a theatrical device, it was only a partial success.

Instead of sending those little kiddies reeling back in shock-horror at the close proximity of a bloodthirsty pirate gang, our theatrical technique invoked a barrage of boos and insults. During the Saturday afternoon performance in particular, one little kid even spat at me to express his disdain for my thespian efforts to entertain him. Taking a cue from their chum, a couple of his pals leapt from their seats and attacked the other members of the pirate gang with their bunched fists.

For a moment, I wished that my wooden cutlass had had a honed edge of Toledo steel. So armed, I would gladly have carved out the little brat's salivary glands. Unfortunately, there wasn't time for any retaliation from the pirate gang, because there was far too much stage "business" to perform.

In the absence of any proper wings to the Town Hall stage, we had rehearsed the return to our off-stage positions by leaving the building via the huge flight of steps onto Long Causeway. Once there, we'd dashed right round the Town Hall and re-entered the building via a side-door on Manor Street. A short sprint up a couple of flights of stairs, and we were soon back-stage, awaiting our next entry cue.

But all such business had been rehearsed during long, dark evenings when the town centre streets had been more-or-

... attacked the pirate gang with their bunched fists.

less deserted. Now, on a December Saturday afternoon, many Christmas shoppers are somewhat taken aback as Long John Silver, complete with tricorn hat, wooden leg and accompanying crutch, dashes breathlessly down the Town Hall steps. All Long John's fellow pirates are "ooh arring" for all their worth as they follow Mr Producer's instructions to maintain their theatrical characters - "for the publicity"- on a full circuit of the Town Hall.

Meanwhile, back on stage, the wily Ben Gunn [Archie Madden] emerges from the wings to face the audience of kiddies. He confides in them that he is about to lift the pirate treasure from its pretend hole, which LJS and his Men had been "unable" to find. And whilst the rest of the pirate gang are away enjoying their *al fresco* trip on Long Causeway, Ben Gunn informs his audience that he is about to leave a solitary coin in place of the treasure. He creeps off-stage, gleefully chortling to himself at his cunning jape.

As pirates, upon our return to the stage, we are about to find out about the missing millions.

Now, the script dictated that Yours Truly [as the pirate George Merry] was to be first into the hole. I was to discover the lack of treasure therein and to find but "one doubloon" remaining.

During rehearsals, this scene and its intricate stage manoeuvres had all run smoothly. Archie [Ben Gunn] had dutifully left a single coin in the bottom of the hole after removing the precious treasure, and this allowed me [George Merry] to proceed with my exasperated, cheated pirate's diatribe about the consequent lack of financial reward, as indicated in the script:

MERRY:[stoops and picks up a single coin] Two guineas! Two guineas! Is that your seven hundred thousand pounds? Is that your fortune?

However, on this particular occasion during the Saturday afternoon matinée, Ben Gunn had decided to indulge in some Archie Madden-devised mischief.

Upon discovering that our hole is devoid of treasure, at this moment of tense theatrical drama, the pirate George Merry leaps into the hole. He looks down, expecting to find the single coin left by Ben Gunn. Instead he finds a succinct, hand-written message from Archie Madden. It is a single sheet of foolscap paper which bears the legend in large capital letters:

"BOLLOCKS, FRED!"

George Merry's subsequent speech about the missing treasure is delivered through clenched teeth as he strives to suppress a fit of stage giggles...

A moment of pure Madden Magic occurred very recently at the Arts Group's own premises on Lower Peel Street in Dewsbury.

During an evening of One-Act Plays, Archie is portraying the character of Monsieur Cliquot in a comic one-acter by Galton and Simpson. The first of the three plays in the programme is well under way and the cast of the next offering on the bill - "Cliquot et Fils" - is gathering in the bar-area, preparatory to taking the stage. Absolutely no noise must emanate from this assembled group. After all, the watching audience is but six feet away on the other side of a fairly thin wall.

Ten or so characters, male and female and all in costume, tip-toe into the room. In undertaker's black weeds, Archie shuffles along in their midst. Conversations are tense and hushed; first night nerves promote only the quietest of whispers amongst the cast. The atmosphere is nervously silent.

Somebody - to this day, unidentified - breaks wind. It is a deep, resonant trump, heard by all those present.

Silent glances of disapproval are exchanged amongst all members in the room. One or two of the ladies hoist their shoulders in disdainful disgust. Others cluck their disapproval, but no-one present issues an apology for committing such an anti-social biological function. Nobody owns up to that Diabolical Anatomical Act.

It is left to Archie to relieve the tension of the atmosphere in his own typical style.

He peers enquiringly over the top of his theatrical pince-nez at the gathering. With an aged look of resignation, he asks in hushed tones: "Did somebody tread on a frog?"

Amateur thespian activities continued to furnish me with Shoddy Town laughs galore over the years. School pantomimes, written and performed alongside my greatest teaching pal, David Moss, gave me licence to indulge my pathetic aspirations to become a comic actor, and I even developed enough confidence to branch out into other areas of the local entertainment industry...

By 1980, I'd appeared in several Arts Group productions and had seen Russell Whiteley's hugely entertaining and comic renditions of Stanley Holloway monologues, performed at regular Music Hall evenings. Russell would dress up in an Edwardian costume, don a tricorn hat, remove his false teeth and deliver his version of "Gunner Joe".

I noted that people at such events would collapse in side-splitting mirth even before Russell opened his mouth to recite, such was his ability to steer an audience. At that point in my thespian career, I decided that perhaps *I* might be able to perform in like vein.

There is no better nor rewarding feeling than that generated by the sound of audience laughter which *you* alone have managed to elicit. This notion was one that I'd applied to my classroom practice on almost a daily basis, working on the premise that children who are having fun in the classroom will also learn better. Eventually, in order to instil moral values into my young adolescent charges, I'd even extended the idea to my school assemblies, whenever my turn came round to take one.

In the school hall at Earlsheaton, I enjoyed "captive" audiences of both adults and children. After all, the kids were hardly likely to get up and walk out of either classroom or assembly hall because the "act" was sub-standard. The teachers may have considered the idea, but generally shrank from actually doing so in case they themselves might be button-holed to take assemblies in the future.

So I had free rein to "entertain" under the guise of educational practice. As ripples of laughter ran through my assembly audiences, so my confidence grew. Revelling in the ego-boosting emotions generated by raising a laugh, I eventually jumped in at the deep end. Before a school concert in 1978, I plucked up courage and offered an act which included a Stanley Holloway monologue entitled "Gunner Joe".

The Parent-Teacher Association concert organisers almost bit off my Shoddy Town hand. Before I knew it, I was facing a mixed audience of children and grown-ups, and the curtain has once again shot up.

Dressed as a sailor in a ridiculously small costume and wearing large, black wellington boots, I tell a few jokes and recite my monologue to an accompaniment of background piano music provided by Kath Rochell, the school's music teacher. I plod through the recitation of "Gunner Joe", mimicking the style of Russell Whiteley, and I get a few laughs in the right places. At the end of my act, a sympathetic audience applauds my efforts politely, and I leave the stage.

By the summer of 1980, I was mis-reading the entire theatrical scenario as a result of my misguided conceit.

For a couple of years, several local audiences had all politely applauded my efforts to entertain, and my ego-trips in front of assembly children had continued. Feeling full of my own self-importance and visualising a career in show business which would render me a household name throughout the country, I was sure that now was the time to unleash my act on an unsuspecting Shoddy Town public. I would become famous overnight, leave the teaching profession far behind, over yonder on a distant horizon, and make my star-struck way to London, New York and the World. I might even appear on the telly...

And how does one make the inevitable break-through into the world of comedy entertainment? Well, in the absence of variety theatres, I discovered that the way to advance my thespian career lay on the Working Men's Clubs circuit of the Heavy Woollen District.

The method turned out to be quite simple. All you had to do was telephone the Concert Secretary of any of the local clubs and ascertain when the next Monthly Audition Night was to be held. I discovered that you should turn up and perform your act before an audience of members and local area Concert Secretaries. Any of these assembled Concert Secretaries who liked what they saw would then offer you engagement dates [and appearance money] at their respective clubs. And your life in show-biz starts here!

So with a head twice its normal size and an ego which was over-inflated to gas-balloon size, I prepared manfully to go over the top into the No Man's Land of show business as The World Famous "Gunner Joe". This was it!

A balmy June evening in 1980 finds me drawing up in my battered old Vauxhall Viva outside Blackwyke Working Men's club, down a ginnel off a main road, somewhere in the Heavy Woollen District.

The long, low red-brick building casts a sombre shadow across the car-park which is little more than a medium-sized back-yard. Separated from the busy highway by rows of Victorian terraced houses, this yard rarely basks in any Shoddy Town sunlight so the entrance to the club remains in constant gloom. With all the attributes of an abandoned bakery, the Working Men's Club presents a daunting facade to the newcomer on the entertainment circuit. I note from my watch that it's now ten minutes to my audition time

As I sit in my car contemplating my next move, first night

nerves have begun to tear violently at my stomach muscles and lower bowel area.

I could easily turn tail, drive home to Batley and mark a pile of exercise books which await my attention on our living-room table. Or I could leave my sailor suit in the boot and enter the building *incognito* just to witness the scene, before finally deciding that this was not a suitable venue for Gunner Joe's first professional appearance on stage. Or perhaps I could drive round for a while and then return home after an hour or two to tell everyone that I'd searched the district high and low but hadn't been able to find Blackwyke Working Men's Club *anywhere*.

However, after five minutes' mental and physical anguish, I decided to bite the bullet. Screwing up every last morsel of my courage and quivering like the leaves on a wind-swept tree, I grabbed my kit and mounted the wide, stone steps in the corner of the gloomy yard.

Through the dark, wooden double-doors I crept diffidently into a dimly lit hallway where a free-standing notice-board bore a large, hand-written notice:

TONITE
LOCAL AUDITIONS NITE
ADMISSION FREE   ALL WELCOME
Members please note: No pie and peas will be served

Swallowing hard, I plucked up courage to open another set of doors and to make my way into a long, dark concert room.

Spread around the floor, there were many of the usual WMC round tables, each with its set of three or four dark wooden chairs. At the far end, across a red-and-black, vinyl-tiled floor-area stood a small, gloomy stage - the setting for my impending burst onto the show-biz scene.

To my left was a long, dimly-lit bar, the entrance to which was a sort of archway behind some supporting pillars. Behind the bar, an ageing, bald little man in a lime-green waistcoat, wearing half-moon spectacles on the end of his nose, was busy filling shelves with bottles of Webster's "Green Label". I decided to make him my first point of contact.

Nervously making my way under the archway, I leant over the bar top. "Er...excuse me, sir," I stammered.

But before I could announce the purpose of my mission, Mr Barman leapt up and craned his neck towards me. "T'bar's shut, owd lad. We dooan't open wol eight on t'audition neets. Nob'dy's bothered, tha sees." And he disappeared down below to continue his shelf-filling.

"Well.... er.... actually," I ventured, straining over the bar and peering into the dark depths below. "As a matter of fact, I've come to take an active part in the audition..."

I was making full use of Standard Teacher Speak, feeling that a Star of Tomorrow ought to show some sense of decorum and propriety. I continued above the rattle and clatter of beer-bottles: "I wondered if you might be able to direct me to the Artistes' Changing Room where I might deposit my costume."

Reminiscent of Mr Punch, Mr Barman jack-in-a-boxed over the bar top.

"Oh, tha'r one o' t'turns, ar' ta? Well, tha should 'a' sed. Tha'r a bit ter sooin, owd cocker. We dooan't kick off wol 'alf-past eight, tha knows. Any rooad, tha's ter see t'Concert Secretary over yonder - through yon door."

He indicated a dark corner at the side of the stage where there was another dark, little door, before he dived once more out of sight, down below the bar.

Still shaking with fear in what seemed like every sinew of my thespian body, I shambled miserably across to the said door, as indicated by Mr Barman. I respectfully knocked, paused and nervously pushed it open.

In a dingy little room with high windows and all the trappings of a Dickensian office, behind a low wooden desk, sat another ageing, balding little fellow with glasses on the end of his nose. However, whilst bearing a very strong resemblance to Mr Barman, this chap's waistcoat was a sombre navy-blue.

My Inner Voice whispered to me in Shoddy Town Speak: "*'Appen's this is t'other feller's brother.*"

Surrounded by plastic money-bags bulging with coins and an array of bank notes, Mr Barman's Brother was writing carefully in a large black ledger on the desk in front of him. Clearly, he was unaware of my presence in the room.

I coughed nervously and announced my arrival, reverting to Standard Teacher Speak: "Good evening, sir. I'm here for an audition and was told to report to you."

Mr Barman's Brother looked up, startled. A look of sheer panic flashed across his face and, in a desperate attempt to conceal the cash in front of him, he threw his entire upper body across the desk, scattering paper and money-bags onto the floor. He continued our consultation in this spread-eagled, semi-prone position.

He peered up at me, over the rim of his half-moon spectacles. "Tha'r a bit ter sooin, owd lad," he muttered, echoing his brother's reply of a few minutes ago. "We dooan't kick off wol 'alf-past."

Still sprawled across his desk with arms outstretched to conceal last night's takings, he nodded towards a door across the other side of the dimly lit room. It was slightly ajar.

"Get thisen through theer, cocker," he instructed. "Ah'm nobbut t'Club Treasurer. Tha wants Maurice. 'E's t'Concert Secretary an' 'e's in t'Artistes' Room. It's 'im as tha needs ter see."

Still wracked by trembling fear and quivering from head to toe, I entered a smaller but brightly lit room with a large floor-standing mirror in the far corner. Reflected in it, I see yet another carbon copy of Mr Barman/Mr Treasurer. This one turns his ageing, balding head towards me to reveal a rather flamboyant plum-coloured waistcoat.

Peering at me over the rim of his half-moon spectacles, he wrinkles the end of his nose in enquiring fashion: "What's ta want, owd lad? It's "artistes only" in 'ere, tha knows."

Throwing all decorum to the Four Winds, I lapse into exasperated Shoddy Town Speak: "Aye, Ah know. Yond feller in theer told me to repoort ter thee. If tha'r Maurice, Ah'm Gunner Joe."

"Oh, tha'ar, ar ta? Well, tha'r a bit ter sooin, owd lad - we dooan't kick off wol 'alf-past. But tha'r in t'reight place."

"Ah'm t'feller as tha wants - Maurice Bickerdyke, t'Concert Secretary. Pleased ter meet thi, cocker. Tha mun sit thisen dahn a minit or two."

With a nod, he indicated a small brown chair beside the free-standing mirror.

By now, my nerves are so stretched that I'm sure their jangle can be heard the length and breadth of the entire club. I throw my sailor suit over the chair in a corner of the cramped dressing-room and nervously perch my bum on its edge.

After a few minute's perusal of a sheet in front of him, Maurice turns to me. He clears his throat and adopts an official-sounding tone: "Nahthen, lad. Wi me bein' t'Concert Secretary, Ah've ter soort one or two things aht. So Ah 's'll 'ave to ask thi a very important question, an' it's this: 'When will ta be gooin' on?'"

Interpreting this to be a reassuring Shoddy Town enquiry about my general well-being and state of health, as in "*Nahthen, lad, 'ow ar ta gooin' on?*", I replied in like vein: "Ah'm nooan ser bad, thanks. Shekkin' a bit wi' t'nerves, tha knows, burr Ah's'll be awreight in a bit."

For Maurice, this was a completely nonsensical reply. Furrows of doubt began to knit his balding brow in consternation and he began to think that he was dealing with a thespian crackpot.

As Concert Secretary, Maurice was responsible for completing a running order of the acts for the Audition Night entertainment. His question to me had been an attempt to ascertain my preferred position in the programme of events.

Now, what I didn't know then, but discovered later, was that prime spot on audition nights was *always* early on in the evening. Appearing at number one or two in the running order meant that aspiring performers would get through their acts before the assembled gathering of Concert Secretaries had had chance to consume vast quantities of ale [at WMC prices].

In addition, any other members of the audience who had taken advantage of the free admission [without pie or peas] would only be present for the purposes of ale-consumption, not giving a tinker's curse for the acts on the stage in front of them. Budding artistes were thus well advised to get their appearances in early, before beer began to cloud the judgement of the assembled crowd in waves of alcoholic fug.

Screwing up his nose and giving me a look of doubtful disbelief, Mr Concert Secretary corrects my misinterpretation of his enquiry.

"Nay, owd cock. Tha's got me wrong. Worr Ah meean is: "What number dusta want ter be on t'bill? Ah meean ter say, when will ta be gooin' on - early or late?"

Naively and seeking to be polite, I decline a decision:

"Nay lad. Ah dooan't know. It's up to thee. Ah'll goo on whenever tha wants."

"Oh, reight then," replies Maurice eagerly. "Tha can goo on at ten, after t'novelty act." And he heaves a sigh of relief. He has just filled the "graveyard spot" on his bill with no bother at all. Beaming the smile of a man who has backed a 33-1 winner, he continues with organisational matters.

"Yon door over theer is thi entrance on to t'stage." He

nodded towards a small door in the corner of the room. "An' tha wants ter bi theer three or fower minits afore tha'r due on. Nahthen, dusta 'ave any music wi' thi?"

"Aye, Ah 'ave that," I reply, and I delve into the pocket of my sailor suit to proudly produce a musical score - the accompaniment to my monologue: "*to be played at a moderate/slow pace, in time with the recitation.*"

"Oh, reight then - so tha'll need ter 'ave a word wi Clarrie, t'pianist. 'E's aht theer, in t'Room." Maurice nods in the direction of the Concert Room through yet another door in the Artistes' Quarters.

So I'd now completed a full circuit of the building, or so it seemed, because I passed through the door as instructed to find myself back in the Concert Room. Shading my eyes from the relatively brighter lights, I cast a look round and notice Mr Clarrie Pianist busy opening up the lid of a large piano at the foot of the stage steps.

Positioned immediately below the level of the stage, Clarrie's seated body allows his ageing, balding head to just peep over the edge of the stage. He takes a seat on his piano stool and adjusts his half-moon spectacles. Pulling down his maroon waistcoat, he stretches out his arms before running his bony fingers over the ivories.

As I make my way over, I can't help thinking that the entire staff of the club are in some way related to each other, such are the similarities in their appearances and modes of dress. Perhaps Clarrie is a cousin of the other three.

I sidle nervously up to the side of the piano and give a muffled cough to announce my arrival.

Clarrie looks up from the keyboard and spies the sheet of music in my hand.

"Ey oop! A customer! Tha'r a bit ter sooin, owd lad. We dooan't kick off wol 'alf-past, tha knows."

"Ah know. Everybody an' 'is mother's telled me that," I retort. But Clarrie is not listening as he makes a grab for my music.

"What's ta got theer," he mutters and he peers at the page before him.

Now that I am nearer [by about twenty minutes] to actually taking the stage, and feeling that it is more in keeping with theatrical appearances, I lapse back into Standard Teacher Speak:

"That's the musical score to accompany my monologue," I explain. "As you can see, it needs to be played at a slow and moderate pace. Now, I'm not actually due to appear until ten o'clock, so if you'd like to run through it beforehand, I'd be more than happy to oblige.

Clarrie Pianist looks at me incredulously. "Nay lad! Ah 'aven't time ter be runnin' through owt wi' anybody. Ah've ter tek some wet fish 'ooam to t'wife for mi supper afore Ah kick off 'ere. Just thee leave this wi' me. It'll be reight."

Standing up and shoving the piano-stool underneath the key board, he stuffs my sheet-music into his back pocket, before shambling off towards the door marked 'EXIT'.

As he disappears into the Big Wide World outside, I cannot help but worry. During the next ten minutes or so, my sheet of music, a vital part of my act, could well end up wrapped around a piece of Mrs Clarrie's slimy wet haddock. But there's little I can do about it now, so I shrug my shoulders and make my desolate way to a seat at the back of the Concert Room.

I sit on my chair in the corner, glance at my watch and note that I still have aeons of time before I am to appear before the Blackwyke general public. I am just about to seek out Mr Concert Secretary to ask his permission to stay out front for a while but I'm startled back into my seat by the arrival of the other would-be Stars of Tomorrow.

I gape, open-mouthed, as a succession of audition night hopefuls traipses past me on their separate ways to the Artistes' Room.

Through the far door, a hugely rotund lady with raven hair and heaving bosom bursts in. She announces to anybody who might be listening that she is "first on" and she makes for the Artistes' Room door. She is followed by a thin, wizened little man in his forties sporting a striped waistcoat and trailing an equally thin, wizened little mongrel behind him.

Next in is a young, fair-haired lad with a red face, a tape recorder and a microphone stand. He makes a bee-line for my table, mistaking me for someone important in the Blackwyke WMC hierarchy of club management.

"Ah'm t'comedy turn, me. Ah'm bloody funny, me, tha knows. Ah can mek owt laugh, me. Wheer shall Ah set up mi gear, owd cock?"

I open my mouth to put tonight's comedy act right on a few things, but my reply is stifled in its tracks by the arrival of the final audition act. The double doors burst open again and a large black suitcase crashes in, followed by a thin angular chap with a high domed forehead and a limp. He is tonight's novelty act, I discover, so I've a vested interest in him because my act follows his in the running order.

I cast a furtive look round the assembled motley crew of theatrical hopefuls and wonder what on earth I am doing in their midst. I'm just about to call the whole thing off when Mr Concert Secretary calls us all together to inform us of arrangements for the evening's auditions.

"Nahthen, let's be seein'," he mumbles as he consults a hastily written scrap of paper in his hand.

"Yer runnin' order for terneet is: First: Normanton Nell and her Songs from the Shows; second: Billy Bottomley and Jack, the Performing Pup; third: Charlie Chuckle, Yorkshire's Funniest Man; fourth: Henry and His Amazing Harmonicas; and last: Gunner Joe. Best o' luck ter y'all."

With a smug smile of satisfaction, he turns away resignedly and makes for the bar which is now open for business. "Mine's a pint, Clarrie," he calls to Mr Pianist, who has just returned hot-foot from the fish-shop. With some relief, I notice that my sheet-music is still poking out of his back pocket.

Well, there was *no* going back now. A few people had begun to trickle into the Concert Room for their night's free entertainment; the bar was open; the running order had been set. To turn tail and run now was an impossibility.

I made my trembling way with the others into the Artistes' Room. In the subsequent general mêlée of preparations for the impending auditions, I discover that my neatly folded sailor's suit has been flung into a corner and that Jack the Performing Dog has claimed it for his bed. Normanton Nell now occupies the chair upon which my costume had been placed, and she is currently daubing a variety of colours onto her face.

I shoo away Jack the Performing Dog and rescue my costume. As I dust it off, I stand, insignificantly in the corner where it had been flung, and witness the WMC entertainment scene from a detached stand-point.

There is a quiet hum of conversation as preparations for the coming session continue. In the centre of the room, firmly ensconced on her chair with lipstick and mirror in hand, Normanton Nell turns to Billy Bottomley. "'Ey oop, Bill! Did yer go ter t'auditions at 'Eckmondwike last week?"

"Aye, Ah did," replies Billy, fondly stroking Jack's wiry back. "Burr ar Jack 'ere lerrus dahn. Pee'd on one o' t'footleets 'alf way through t'act, 'e did, an' it started a fire."

"What 'appened," enquired Nell, disinterestedly.

"Oh, nowt much. T'Concert Secretary - tha knows, 'im wi t'wooden leg - 'e purr it aht wi' a fire extinguisher. There were an 'oggin o' smoke, burr it wor awreight after half-an-'our. They 'adn't ter call t'fire-brigade or shut t'bar or owt like that. They kept servin' all t'way through."

"Good job Ah couldn't gooa, then," retorts Nell, poking at her eye-lashes with what looked like a decorator's half-inch paint-brush. "Ah 'ad ter see ter mi mother's cat, y'know. She dun't gerr abaht like she used ter, so Ah 'ad ter tek 'er shoppin' in mi basket ."

"What? Tek thi mother shoppin in thi basket?" Billy

scratches the back of his head and knits a puzzled brow.

"Is she a bit on a dwarf, then, thi mother?"

Meanwhile, Charlie Chuckle the comedian with his ear about an inch away from the speaker, is bending over his tape-recorder listening intently and desperately attempting to "cue it up" for his impending act. Above the hum of surrounding conversation, he plays and replays the same snatches of tape-recorded sounds, timing being of obvious vital importance. The sounds of telephone rings, an explosion or two and a huge splash of water emanate from the speaker. I ponder the prospect of all these sounds fitting into his act as the Funniest Man in Yorkshire, but my pondering is brought to an abrupt halt as Henry the Harmonica Man opens his suitcase with a flourish.

Reaching down, he extracts the biggest, shiniest mouth-organ I have ever clapped eyes on. It as at least three feet wide and Henry has all on to lift it up to his pursed lips for a quick trill up and down the scales. After a couple of minutes, his combined efforts to hold up the considerable weight of his instrument along with his attempts to blow into it, render his face the colour of a ripe Victoria plum. Eventually, he collapses into a vacant chair, his chest heaving as he desperately gasps for life-giving oxygen.

Throughout the past few minutes, my attention has been totally absorbed in the varying activities of my fellow artistes. I stare at them in gob-smacked wonder and again question the reason for my own presence in such bizarre company. Whilst I ponder, I have failed to notice the relentless progress of the clock which is ticking towards kick-off time.

The muffled tinkling of the ivories drifts in from the Concert Room as Clarrie the Pianist warms up the assembled audience. Mingling with the strains of "Side Saddle" on the piano, there is the audible chink of glasses and the occasional raucous guffaw from beyond the doors of our Artistes' Room. And with these sounds, my trembling, first night nerves return with a vengeance.

I creep over to the chair vacated by Normanton Nell and park my nethers in a forlorn attempt to quell the shuddering shakes which once again wrack my entire torso. There's a good hour and a half before Gunner Joe is due on stage, by which time both he and I will be shivering wrecks. I have just decided that the pair of us ought to go out front for a stiff drink when the clock catches up with us.

The hub-bub from the Concert Room diminishes as Les "Your Compère" leaves his table of drinking mates, grabs a microphone and clears his throat for an announcement.

Meanwhile, Normanton Nell [first on tonight's bill] ambles over to the door of our tiny room and holds her ear close to it, listening for her cue.

Nonchalantly smoothing down her flame red ball-gown, she continues the conversation about her mother's cat with Billy Bottomley: "Aye, Ah 'ad ter tek it ter t'vets ter 'ave it newted. Ee, it wor a mess though! Blood all over t'shop..."

Billy shakes his head in amazement but before he can add to the conversation, Compère Les in the Concert Room completes his announcement: "Laze an Gen'l'men, the best of order, if you please. Now, as yer know, there's ner pie 'n' peas on terneet, so yer'll 'a' ter mek do wi' crisps an' what-

'ave-yer. Also, if yer've got yer tickets fer this comin' Sat'day neet, yer'll find t'artistes pinned to t'notice-board in our entrance-'all. And now, wi'out further ado, your first act this Audition Neet is "Songs from the Shows" and the lovely Normanton Nell..."

As soon as she catches her cue, Nell abandons her chat with Billy, opens the door and makes a sweeping entrance onto the stage. To a fairly muted ripple of applause, she and Clarrie Pianist launch into a brassy rendition of "*I'm gonna wash that man right out of my hair*".

By now, I am thoroughly miserable. In matters theatrical, I realise just how wet-behind-the-ears I actually am. My tasteful, Edwardian drawing-room act of gentle recitation has little place in this brash, glitzy show-biz world of singers and novelty acts. But I am trapped in a situation of my own making and there's no escape. I *must* proceed.

I creep out of the Artiste's Room exit door, down a corridor and through the double doors at the back of the Concert Room.

An audience of some fifty or so people has gathered and amongst them, there are several older chaps with notebooks on the table in front of them, beside their pint glasses. These are the massed ranks of the Shoddy Town Concert Secretaries, on the look-out for the new and rising talent of the Heavy Woollen District. At the moment, none of them looks too impressed with Nell's rendition of "*There's a place for us*".

As I slink unnoticed into a seat in the shadows at the back, Nell reaches the crowning touch to her act with a rising crescendo in "*My way*" and she bows low to leave the stage.

There is hardly any applause as several audience members take their cues to dash to the bar, just before Compère Les grabs the microphone, half-full pint glass in hand.

"An' now, laze an' gen'l'men, as usual, there will be an interval of ten minutes." He drains his pint, deposits the microphone on the edge of the stage and makes for the corner of the bar where a full pint glass already awaits his attention.

I hunch my shoulders over the table in front of me in the anonymous safety of the shadows. It is barely nine o'clock . Over an hour left...

By the time Billy Bottomley has persuaded Jack to demonstrate his extraordinary canine abilities, the attention span of the watching crowd has dwindled noticeably. Extended pauses in Billy's act, during which Jack ceases his yapping to relieve himself several times behind a loudspeaker, have "lost" the audience. There is a steady trickle of people to and from the bar mirrored by a similar procession to and from the toilets at the back of the Concert Room. The free admission factor has begun to kick in, allowing, as it did, for more than the usual amount of hard-earned Shoddy Town cash to be spent on alcohol consumption.

Perhaps the introduction of Yorkshire's Funniest Man will stem the tide of movement, I think to myself, as Charlie Chuckle takes to the stage, tape-recorder at the ready. But as his act proceeds, I become even more depressed.

Each and every of Charlie's remarks is liberally sprinkled with a generous helping of the "F..." word, and a steady flow of invective sarcasm is the feature of the next ten minutes or so. Every other word in the act is one of those which are "taboo" in my own daily working life and for which I would be severely punished if I were to be caught using them. I fear for the bland, drawing-room naivety of my act by comparison. I sink even lower in my seat and I hold my head in my hands.

Glancing up, I see that the clock has once again caught up with me. It's time to make my way back-stage and change into my show-biz costume. As Henry the Harmonica Man drags his suitcase onto the stage, I trudge dismally back to the Artistes' Room, desperately rehearsing the lines of my monologue under my breath.

Climbing into my silly sailor's short trousers, I consider spicing up the first few anecdotes of my act with the "F..." word, but decide that, at this late stage, such a ploy would only throw me. In front of this audience, already full to the gunwales with ale, it would represent theatrical suicide. No, there was nothing for it but to proceed as planned and get the whole miserable affair over as soon as possible.

Still optimistically harbouring the hope that some of those Concert Secretaries out front might recognise *real* thespian talent when it appeared before them, I crept over to the stage entrance door. Levering it carefully ajar, I was able to catch a glimpse of Henry's Amazing Harmonicas novelty act through the slight gap.

Now, as it happened, this novelty act was quite entertaining.

With a theatrical flourish, Henry produced his three-foot harmonica from his suitcase and held it aloft for all to see. He then proceeded to slide his saliva-sodden lips up and down the blow-holes in an up-tempo version of "Ghost Riders in the Sky". At the end of the sequence, he bowed dramatically. Rummaging anew in his suitcase, he produced an exact replica of his three foot instrument, but this one was about a foot shorter.

Over the next ten minutes, peering through my little peephole at the side of the stage, I am utterly enthralled as Henry produces harmonicas of ever-decreasing size from his suitcase, holds them aloft for the audience's brief perusal, and then delivers his tuneful rendition.

The grand finale of the act sees Henry hold aloft a one-inch version of the said wind-instrument. He inserts this tiny harmonica bodily into his mouth and the strains of "Ghost Riders" is only just audible above the rattle of beer-glasses and the general chatter of the Concert Room.

Still amazed at my peep-hole, I fear for Henry's safety. As his face reaches a deep purple hue in the effort to create any audible sound from the tiny instrument within his mouth, I am certain that Henry has swallowed the thing whole.

However, I am halted in my dash on stage to deliver the kiss of life as Henry removes the apparatus from his mouth with another dramatic flourish, takes a bow to the slightest ripple of applause, and drags his suitcase towards the stage exit. He pushes past me through the Artistes' Room door, still quite crimson in the face as a result of his efforts.

"That wor f....... 'oss work," he mutters to no-one in particular, and collapses into a chair on the other side of the room.

Meanwhile, back in the Concert Room, Compère Les has once again taken up the microphone for an announcement. He staggers to the front of the stage and leans casually on the piano. There is quite a pause as he summons up the ability to speak.

By now, the audience is in no desperate need whatsoever of any break in proceedings. Beer glasses are sufficiently filled, thank you very much, tonight's auditions are very nearly over, and it's about time to leave for home. Les, like his audience, is not only well-charged with Webster's Green Label, he is also keen to get the whole affair over and done with.

At last, he clears his throat for a drunken announcement of the final act.

"Yer final turn, thish evenin', laze an' gen'l, the besht order pleeeez... for..."

Swaying like a sapling in a gale, he runs his wayward finger down his list and peers closely at it, his nose but two inches from the page.

"Nah, lesh 'ave a shee... Oh aye, 'ere we are: The besht order fo' terneet's last act: Gunter John. I thank yooo, laze an' gen..." And he collapses into a chair.

In the Artistes' Room, expecting another ten-minute break between acts, I have been completely taken by surprise. Yanking on my sailor's top and shoving my feet desperately into my wellies, I stumble on stage and make a dash for the centre.

"*You'll be fine,*" my Inner Voice tells me in Standard Teacher Speak. "*The first few bars of slow, deliberate introduction to your monologue will give you time to pull yourself together.*"

But Clarrie Pianist has other ideas. Relishing the thought of a nice bit of haddock for his supper, he sets off on the "slow and moderate" introduction like an express train, his gnarled old fingers fairly whizzing up and down the ivories.

I am completely thrown. Mouth agape, I face my inebriated audience. Every back is turned towards me in apathetic disdain as I forget my first line and have to bend down to Clarrie to ask for a prompt.

"What's mi first line," I hiss desperately.

"Eh? Tha wot?" asks exasperated Clarrie who is now playing my accompaniment in over-drive and who is extremely keen to get home for his haddock.

"'Ow does it start," I almost shout through clenched teeth.

Clarrie screams to a halt and peers at the sheet music. "Thi first line...let's 'ave a see..."

He looks up at me with a frown. "It's a bugger is this, tha knows. Ah's'll be late fo' mi supper. T'wife'll think Ah'm gassed ageean." And he returns to his search of my music.

Feeling the acutest embarrassment at my ineptitude in front of an audience, I pray for a cavernous hole to open in the floor of the stage down which I might bolt to safety. I risk a glance upwards as Clarrie cleans his spectacles before continuing his investigation into my missing line.

None of the audience seems to be the slightest bit concerned about my theatrical uselessness. Huddled round their tables piled high with empty glasses, they continue to ignore me as they laugh drunkenly at their own humorous remarks. I look out on rows of turned backs.

At last, Clarrie finds my missing line. "It sez 'ere," he announces to me, "*I'll tell you a sea-faring story of a lad who won honour and fame*" That's thi first line, cocker. Nar gerron wi' it, young 'un. Then we can all gerroff 'ome."

I stumble dismally through the monologue and tell a few lame jokes. Nobody laughs and nobody applauds my exit. I am the World's Most Relieved Man to get it all over and done with, yet at the same time The Most Dismal.

My show-biz career lies about me in shattered fragments on the floor of the Artistes' Room at Blackwyke WMC as the realisation dawns that there will be no Concert Secretary throughout all the Shoddy Towns who will be remotely interested in Gunner Joe as a promising, prospective act.

Ashen-faced and feeling utterly wretched, I change into my everyday clothes and prepare to leave.

I am in need of a stiff drink to bolster my severely deflated theatrical ego, and I make my way along the dark corridor from the Artistes' Room towards the exit. The best place for me at this point is at home with a bottle. But as I pass the entrance to the Concert Room, my Inner Voice attempts to reassure me in Shoddy Town Speak: "*Well, tha never knows. One o' t'Concert Secretaries might be waitin' aht theer ter give thee a bookin'. It's worth a look, i'n't it?*"

Feeling slightly better, I experience a faint, late surge of optimism. After all, my act hadn't been all *that* bad, had it?

"*Goo on,*" encourages my Inner Voice. "*Gie it a gooa - tha's nowt ter loise, as ta?*"

I decide to respond to such encouraging advice.

Timidly, I venture into the Concert Room to see if any Concert Secretaries have, indeed, recognised the raw theatrical talent of my act. If they have, they'll be waiting in there with their diaries open, ready to offer me a booking.

I creep into the back of the near-empty Concert Room and approach the bar. Leaning heavily on one of the archway pillars is a young, dark-haired chap.

"Perhaps this is a local Concert Secretary who is eager to reserve your services for his club," says my Inner Voice in Standard Teacher Speak. I lean expectantly with both hands on the bar-top.

"Good evening," I announce out loud and very politely, in anticipation of an official approach.

Half-full pint glass in his drunkenly wavering hand, the young man is cross-eyed with drink as he fixes me with a glassy stare. He pushes himself away from the pillar with a super-human effort, swaying violently and spilling beer onto the red-and-black tiled floor.

Screwing up his face, he blinks repeatedly in a drunken effort to focus on me. After half-a-dozen deep breaths and as many false starts, he finally comes out with it:

"By gow, tha wor f...... rubbish terneet, owd lad."

I left Blackwyke WMC shortly afterwards, contemplating the prospect of a pile of exercise-books still to be marked and a thirty year career in teaching...

***

FAR AND  AWAY

One of the delights of a teaching career spent in the company of Shoddy Town lads and lasses was to escape every now and then from the daily classroom routine. Right from the very early days at Batley Boys' High School, any opportunity to flee the school grounds for even the shortest period of time was met with avid enthusiasm by both pupils and their teachers alike.

Not that we teachers looked upon such activity as an easy option. When you're out and about the Shoddy Towns in the company of twenty or thirty young adolescents, *you* are in charge, and what *you* say goes. There's no Headmaster around to oversee your disciplinary decisions or to interfere with the way you do your job. The safety and conduct of the entire shooting-match rests on your shoulders...

"Now tomorrow, boys, we have our long awaited trip to the Bagshaw Museum. A rare delight!"

Dominating the steep slope down to the valley floor and the dust and traffic of Bradford Road, the austere, slated roof of the museum's tower protected a host of historical artefacts from the biting easterly winds as they whipped up from the valley below. And tomorrow, it is to be our privilege to visit that part of our Shoddy Town heritage.

A teacher of some five weeks' full-time experience, I looked down at the thirty pairs of Shoddy Town eyes as they open in wonder and excitement at the prospect of our "trip". Our journey along Upper Batley Lane to Batley's very own museum at the top end of Wilton Park was greeted with the eager, noisy anticipation that only 11 year-olds can muster.

In 1966, all those bright-eyed and enthusiastic First Year lads at Batley High School had been following a Social Studies course, organised by the ebullient, enthusiastic Allen Lawton - Head of Lower School. In those far-off days of mid-60's educational practice, this course was an all-new, all-singing and all-dancing approach to student learning - called "Team Teaching".

In reality, it meant that each member in the team of six teachers took on the teaching and organisation of a theme which was connected in some way to the social history, geography and economic life of our town. Each teacher could therefore deliver "lessons" in his own particular specialism. Mine, I remember, was "Sport in Batley".

In and amongst all the football, rugby and cricket information about Batley which I'd managed to turn up as useful teaching material, I'd also discovered the existence of an old-fashioned game called "knur-and-spell". This had been a leisure-time occupation enjoyed by many generations of Shoddy Town folk in days gone by, so it provided vivid local colour with regard to my chosen theme.

Simple enough in its conception, the game involved whacking a small wooden ball [knur] as far as possible with a long, club-like stick. The winner of any encounter would be the one who could hit that little white ball the furthest.

To facilitate a good hefty whack, the knur was placed into a sprung trap [the spell]. A gentle tap with your club would release the knur up into the air and a good eye was required as you made a lusty swipe at the little round ball on its gravity-driven downward passage to Earth.

And tomorrow, my class and I were going to the Bagshaw Museum to inspect their "knur-and-spell" equipment of bygone days. Perhaps, if I played my smarmy cards right with Mr Curator, we might even be allowed to have a go at the game ourselves!

For the present, I continue, in instruction mode, to provide the class with detailed information regarding arrangements for our "trip".

"Now boys, it's only three-quarters of a mile to the museum, so we shall be walking there, along Upper Batley Lane. We'll leave school at 9.30am prompt. We shall have a look round the museum and then you'll have to draw the knur-and-spell equipment, so bring a pencil. We shall return to school at about 12 o'clock. Now, have you all got that?"

For such a minor "trip", I thought I'd given a fair amount of organisational detail - quite enough for even the greatest of First Year Worriers. But I was wrong.

"Sir," pipes up Holroyd, a thin boy with a centre-parting in his fair hair - and a stickler for detail. "Will Ah need to wear mi shoes or mi pumps?"

Holroyd's question prompts a barrage from the rest of the wide-eyed First year kids:

"Aye, sir. If we've ter walk it, 'ave Ah ter bring mi bus-fare?"

"'Ave we ter bring some snap wi' us, sir, in case we get lost?"

"Aye, reight enough, sir. Mi Dad says Ah've ter bring 'is compass, so as we can find us way back."

"If it rains, sir, will we get wet?"

"*Sir, can we go swimmin'?*"

This last question was one which was to haunt my thirty-years at the chalk-face on almost a daily basis.

On countless numbers of trips far and away from the sunny climes of Bradford Road, I was asked the self-same question in all sorts of varying circumstances and in many different parts of the world. It seemed that the Shoddy Town kids of yester-year were avid devotees of the aquatic hobby and were always prepared for a dip, no matter where they happened to be on the earth's surface.

On one occasion, I was even asked the question at the very foot of the Eiffel Tower by a Batley lad, brandishing a snorkel, with his swimming trunks neatly wrapped in a brown paper-bag stuffed into his back pocket...

But today, in early October 1966, I am taken aback by the flood of trivial questions. In typical inexperienced, wet-behind-the-ears fashion, I attempt to answer each lad's query individually, but am beaten by the ringing of the bell for the first lesson of the day.

"Look, lads," I shout in desperation. "Just meet me outside the Changing Rooms at half-nine tomorrow. Bring whatever you think you'll need." And the boys file out of the classroom for their first lesson of the day.

As they leave, my Inner Voice, confiding privately in Shoddy Town Speak, is professionally amazed: "*We're nobbut walkin' to t'museum on Upper Batley Lane. Tha'd think we wor offter t'Moon...*"

The following morning, at the appointed hour, I make my way to the Changing Room entrance. This is my first "trip" as a fully-fledged teacher, so I must admit to a little tremor of anticipatory excitement myself. Rounding the corner at the top end of the school, I am completely dumbfounded by the sight which met my eyes.

The group of thirty excited lads form a noisy crowd on the yard outside and they have taken yesterday's final instruction to heart.

For a morning's stroll in the pleasant autumn sunshine, young Whitehead has come prepared. He is red-faced and breathless under the load of a bulging rucksack on his back. From it, there hangs a variety of camping paraphernalia. In the fleeting second as I look at him, I catch sight of a tin mug, a pair of binoculars, a map-case and a large, brass compass. He is in earnest conversation with Holderness who is similarly prepared for a mountainous trek in stout walking boots, but who also has a "Brownie" camera slung around his neck.

Next to them, smiling up at me through his tangled mop of tousled black hair, stands "Roly-Poly" Atkinson from Batley Carr. He clutches a small brown suitcase in his left hand and a large plastic lunch- box in his right.

"Mi Mam said Ah might need a bit o' summat t'ayt, sir, so she's put mi up a bit o' snap. Dusta want t' ave a look see, sir?" And he deftly flips open the catches on his suitcase.

"No, Atkinson, lad. It's alright - I believe you, " I reply incredulously as I cast an astounded look round the whole group.

They are all, to a greater or lesser degree, similarly equipped. There are back-packs, satchels and suitcases of varying sizes. Walking-boots seem to be the dominant mode of footwear, although I notice that Robertshaw has come in a pair of brand spanking new wellingtons. One or two heads sport woolly mountain hats and I note that young Sowden has strapped a rolled-up sleeping-bag to the top of his bulging ruck-sack.

Utterly amazed at such a turn-out for our three-quarter mile stroll, my Inner Voice addresses me in professional tones: "*For goodness' sake, we're only going on Upper Batley Lane. Some of these lads are well enough prepared for a Himalayan expedition to Everest.*"

To the assembled gathering of lads, however, my overt remarks are less scornful: "Well, boys, I'm pleased to see that you've come prepared. Holroyd, you *will* take care with that spiked walking stick, won't you. We don't want any-body's eye out, do we? So now, without further ado, let us depart for the Museum."

We set off at a leisurely pace across the football pitch towards the school exit onto Carlinghow Hill. The sun shines, the birds sing and we make our joyful way over the school field - just above the Mud Bath and the infamous Docker Tree of only a few years ago. Column by twos, led by Yours Truly, the Pied Piper, followed by his crowd of Budding Mountaineers as we wend our way into the mists of time gone by...

Throughout my thirty years of teaching, I enjoyed a succes-sion of wonderful school trips when boys and girls showed similar Shoddy Town initiative on their jaunts abroad. Flaunting our motto - "We're fro' Batley/Dewsbury - an' tha can't tell us nowt" - we always made it clear to natives of foreign climes exactly where they stood in our configura-

"...we're only going on Upper Batley Lane"

tion of things. Perhaps people regarded us as strange beings from another planet, but we were always proud to declare our allegiance to our Shoddy Town heritage, no matter where we happened to be.

So as I look back now through my rose-tinted time telescope, I see images and incidents of fun and laughter which took place all over Europe. But the trip which has remained vividly etched on my ageing memory-board takes me back to the halcyon days of 1967...

It was my first tour abroad with a school party, and I was under the protective wing and watchful eye of Milton K. Preston, Head of French at Batley High School. Now Milton was [and still is] an avid enthusiast of the school trip.

Small of stature, the balding Mr Preston was my very first "gaffer" in the teaching profession and he held my utmost respect. With an ability to command the attention of Shoddy Town lads nearly twice his size, from my "rookie's" point of view Milton possessed an almost mystical teaching quality. Boys of all shapes and sizes from all sorts of different backgrounds would accept his every word as gospel and final. They never questioned his decisions in matters of discipline and I remember quite clearly thinking that perhaps one day, I too would be able to command respect in such a way.

So in 1967, it was with a certain sense of pride that I accepted Milton's invitation to join the team on the summer vacation trip to the South of France. We were to spend a fortnight in Cap d'Ail, a summer camp mid-way between Cannes and Nice on the very shores of the Riviera. Our educational responsibility took the form of forty or so

Shoddy Town lads. The team I joined consisted of Milton himself [Team Leader], Allen Lawton [Head of Lower School] and Alan Kitson [Head of Geography].

Looking back, I see now that I was privileged indeed to be on the same coach as three icons of my early teaching career. *These* men had completed their National Service in distant foreign climes, but *I* had been denied the chance by bureaucracy [National Service was scrapped in 1962]. *They* had travelled the globe and had become worldly-wise, whereas *I* had entered teacher training straight from school and still wet behind the ears.

So, with a sense of wonder and awe to be in such company, I boarded the hired coach in the Batley High School drive a couple of days after the 1967 summer holidays had started. I made up the numbers of an excited crowd of Shoddy Town lads of varying ages and four teachers, on our excited way to the "Med."

Our coach-drivers were also men of the world and they operated very much as a team. Eric was tall and swarthy, his dark hair Brylcreemed to glossy perfection. Stanley, on the other hand was freckle-faced, slight of stature and sandy-haired. On the way down the M1, during my front-seat conversation with "our driver" Eric, I discovered that he had been recently roped in to do this particular driving job on Stanley's recommendation to " the gaffer" of the coach-hire firm.

"Ah'm really a JCB driver, tha sees, burr Stan wor stuck fer a mate on this 'ere job, an' t'brass semt awreight, so Ah said Ah'd gie it a gooa," explained Eric, lighting up a Senior Service one-handed at seventy mph. "Me an' Stan's done jobs like this un afore, tha sees, burr not fer three or fower years now..."

Somewhat anxious to hear that our transport-vehicle was to be driven across Europe by a full-time digger-driver, I bite my lip in trepidation. However, reassuring myself that all is well, since these two chaps have "done jobs like this un afore," I settle back into my seat and close my eyes.

A few minutes later, I am wide-eyed and awake as there is noisy activity from the driver's department. I am about to be utterly astounded by the example of Stan 'n' Eric's team-work which takes place just south of Leicester Forest East...

Having driven the coach at regulation motorway speed since leaving Batley, Eric yawns and shouts out to Stanley who has been dozing on the seat behind him.

"Oh, Stan! Gie us a brek, will ta?"

Sleepy Stan returns from the land of Nod immediately. "Aye, O.K. Eric owd lad." And he rises from his seat.

Anticipating a break in our journey while the drivers change shift, I am both somewhat relieved *and* a little puzzled. My relief stems from the fact that I have needed a toilet-stop since Trowell services about twelve miles back, but to my chagrin, we'd shot straight past.

My puzzlement is aroused by my Inner Voice, speaking in relaxed, holiday-spirit, Shoddy Town tones: "'*Ow can we stop nar? Mi bladder's full ter bustin' an' we've just passed t'service station...?*"

My questions are about to be answered in full, as, wide-eyed and mouth agape, I witness the following scenario:

Leaping to his feet and stretching gymnastically, Stan makes his way towards the driver's seat. Eric risks a glance over his shoulder and, at seventy mph, he rises from his seat and moves his torso deftly to one side. Without taking his foot off the accelerator pedal, and with both hands on the steering-wheel, he begins to manouevre himself out of the driver's seat into the gangway next to him, his eyes firmly fixed on the road ahead.

By now, one or two of the lads on the front seats have begun to sit up and take notice. In all their Shoddy Town lives to date, they have never seen such acrobatics at the wheel of a passenger vehicle whilst in motion. And most definitely *never* at seventy mph!

Meanwhile, Stan has begun to squirm under Eric's arms and to take hold of the wheel. Whilst the bus continues its forward trajectory at break-neck speed, Stanley slips his right foot onto the accelerator pedal as Eric slowly removes his . With a quick flick of his rear-end, Stanley slips into the now vacant driver's seat, flaps his nether-regions onto a still-warm cushion [Eric has only been gone for a split second], and the manouevre is complete.

The lads give an appreciative round of applause. The whole operation has taken only a few seconds, during which time, the speed of the bus has not dropped below seventy mph. My urge to visit the toilet has increased at least ten-fold, but now, the next scheduled stop for Rest and Refreshment will have to be at Watford Gap. I cross my legs and wait...

Some hours later, after several mid-journey changes of driver and a couple of very welcome toilet-stops, we arrived at Newhaven, safe, sound and ready to board the cross-channel ferry. This part of our trip was unremarkable enough except for the basic construction of our water-born transport.

As our coach chugged slowly towards the point of embarkation, we noted that the entire front bows of the ship had lifted mechanically into the air above us on some sort of hinged device. Once our vehicle had clanked over the bridge affair between the *terra firma* of Old England and the murky waters of Newhaven harbour, we had to wait several minutes until the bow section had been lowered into place.

There were one or two wide-eyed, first-time-abroad Batley lads in the coach as they watched the bows lower slowly into position to engulf us in the gloom of the lower deck. Shortly after, we were given the all-clear to leave our vehicle, whereupon there was a relieved dash for the safety of the brighter environment on the upper decks.

And so it was at this point in my early teaching career, I learned of Allen Lawton's "man-of-the world" sense of mischief.

Allen was one of the senior members of the Batley High School staff whom I regarded with reverential awe. In his position as Head of Lower School, he commanded instant respect from teachers and boys alike. Mr Lawton was a High School icon to whom we all looked up. Small and stocky, his Lancastrian eyes always had an impish twinkle when he meted out daily discipline to naughty Shoddy Town lads as they went about the school.

Nobody questioned Mr Lawton's decisions about anything because they were always carefully considered, stemming from his sense of fair play and consistent discipline. There was no doubt amongst us that these attributes came naturally to Allen, a lover of Rugby League in general and Widnes in particular.

Imagine then, my first-year teacher's surprise to find that Allen was also a human-being with quite a schoolboy sense of fun. This became immediately apparent as soon as we hit the airy atmosphere of those upper decks and he proceeded to lead us off in the direction of the passenger lounge-bar. Turning to Milton Preston, Allen pulls rank and issues an instruction: "We'll find a seat in the central area of the ship, Milton. That'll probably be the lounge. Come on, before the lads beat us to it."

We three members of staff follow Allen's commanding lead.

"Now, I don't know about you, Fred," he whispered to me confidentially, "but I'm not a sea-faring person. And I have personally discovered that the best thing to combat the rolling and pitching of this here boat is alcohol - and loads of it. Then, you see, sea- sickness or, seeing as we're heading for France, *le mal de mer*, won't be a problem."

"Yes , Mr Lawton, " I nod in respectful agreement.

This was the Head of Lower School issuing an edict, wasn't it? At this stage in my career, who am I to question his pronouncement? I follow meekly in his footsteps to a comfortable seat near a misty port-hole.

A few seconds later, all four of us are sitting in front of a glass of clear liquid, wondering what on earth Allen has bought for our consumption. He sinks into a seat beside me.

"There y'are, Fred - Cointreau. Two or three of these and

you won't even know you're afloat, let alone out on the briny..."

A few hours and several glasses of Cointreau later, a bit of a storm brews up and our ferry begins to pitch and roll in fairly heavy seas. Many passengers are turning a light shade of Lincoln green as the wind and rain batters against the sides of the boat.

In the on-board toilet area, one or two of the boys in the Batley High School party have already parted company with a substantial quantity of their recently gobbled meals.The lounge where we sit is littered with writhing bodies and tortured torsos in the throes of mid-Channel discomfort. At every pitch and roll of the boat, there are accompanying groans of nautical anguish.

However, the teachers in charge of the BHS party have so far performed regular patrols of their charges throughout the journey, and remain strangely unaffected by the crashing up and down and the yawing from side to side of the storm-stricken vessel. Indeed, many passengers marvel at our nautical prowess in maintaining an absolutely straight course during our strolls round the boat, no matter what the angle of the deck beneath our feet.

But keen-eyed observers of the youngest member of staff in charge of the boys may well have noticed that particular teacher's extremely ruddy complexion and his yonderly look. They might also have remarked on his slurred mumblings as he attempted to comfort the sea-sick Shoddy Town lads who appealed to him for assistance in their miserable plight.

"Sir," groans green-faced little first-year Jennings, as I fix him with an inebriated, glassy stare. "All this up an' dahn is mekkin' me gip summat rotten. 'Ow long till we get theer, sir?"

"I have absholootely no ideee, Jenn'ns," I mumble drunkenly. "But wharr I do know is that, in a foo mins time, I sh'll be haccompan'ing Mr Lawton to the resht'rant for a full English breakfasht. All that bacon and egg an' black pudd'n! Mmmm! I'm really looking forward to it." And I lick my lips in delighted relish at the anticipated gastronomic experience.

Peering around through an alcoholic haze, I prepare to offer further words of comfort to young Jennings. But I discover that he has disappeared without trace. From a nearby toilet, there are loud honking noises...

Some two hours and a full English breakfast later, we land in "La Belle France". Our 1967 Batley High School trip to the Riviera unfolds its store of early teaching experiences.

I recall with relish Alan Kitson's boyish delight in observing that he and I "had a French tart" in our Paris hotel bedroom! It became his stock reply in the September staff-room whenever he was talking about our summer holiday trip, and, of course, it raised one or two respectable eye-brows.

After a suitable pause for the general admiration of our men-of-the-world bravado by other members of staff, Alan explained that the "tart" to which he referred had been one of those deliciously sweet "*tarte aux cerises*" available at *la patisserie* not two hundred yards from our hotel.

He and I had been on evening supervision duty and so, while the other adults in our party had been off enjoying the delights of Paris night-life, we sat on the edge of my bed and gorged ourselves on some French confectionery delights not available on Commercial Street or down Branch Road at that time.

And I also remember fondly our Trip Leader's lengthy declarations of his aversion to the French habit of consuming horse-meat in vast quantities.

"If it's horse meat, I'm not touching it. No thank you! It's definitely not for me," Milton kept reminding us for the entire duration of the trip across the Channel.

Eventually, after arrival in Dieppe and thereafter, at whichever establishment we were lodged, we ate communally throughout our stay abroad. We received any dish which was placed on the tables before us with typical Shoddy Town suspicion before hunger took its relentless toll. Lads and teachers alike would then commit themselves to rapid work with knife-and-fork to satisfy the hunger pangs of a long day, no matter what the menu stipulated. As a result, I hit upon a cunning plan to achieve maximum menu satisfaction all the time we were on the French side of the Channel.

Just as the chef's daily offering was placed on the table before us, I would often sniff suspiciously at the appetising plateful deposited in front of Milton. I found it a useful ploy to identify the meat as the abhorrent "*cheval*", whether it was or whether it wasn't.

"Mmm," I'd mutter with a doubtful look on my face. "Looks like horse-meat to me, does that, Milton. Smells like it, too."

"That's it, then," declares Milton. "I'm definitely not touching it. I'll just eat mi vegetables." And, with a look of utter disgust, he slides the succulent meat to one side of his plate.

With an eye for an alimentary extra portion and lapsing into Shoddy Town Speak, I pounce.

"Reight, Ah'll 'ave it then!" Before Milton can reclaim it, I stab greedily with my fork and transfer the offending steak to my plate where I swiftly bury it beneath my pile of "*légumes*" and "*frites*". Such a technique ensured a most satisfactorily full belly throughout the entire trip...

Later on during our southward journey, I was lucky enough to receive further alcoholic tutorship from Allen Lawton one night in Le Puy, a small town in the *Massif Central*. Allen and I had a night off "supervision of lads" duty and so, in the company of Drivers Stan 'n' Eric and our Trip Leader, Milton, we set off for an evening's sight-seeing stroll round the sleepy French town.

Our drivers are as excited as two schoolboys on their first trip abroad. They skip along the cobbled streets, enjoying a night's release from their driver-duties. As the French twilight fades into dusk, they begin to rub their hands together in anticipatory relish.

"Reight, Allen," enthuses Stan. "Worrabaht gerrin' some lotion dahn then, eh?"

"Aye, reight enough, Stan," Eric chimes in agreement. "Ah could reight fancy a pint, Ah could that."

But our Head of Lower School is in educational mood. A man of the world, Allen regards it as his duty to enlighten us all - the young teacher and drivers in his charge - as to the niceties of alcohol consumption whilst we are away from our Shoddy Town habitat. With typical enthusiastic zeal. He sets about his task of teaching us how to drink "*en France*".

"Now this is France, lads, so we'll do our supping like the frogs do. They don't sup pints, Eric, and they don't often sup a great deal of beer."

Eric is crest-fallen and wipes a swarthy hand through his Brylcreemed locks. He has the look of a man who is about to be denied a"neet on t'ale."

"Oh no," continues Allen in teacher-mode. "What they do is find a nice little bar and settle down to drink as many different glasses of lotion as they can. Oh, and there's no bell at closing time, because there isn't one."

Eric is puzzled. "Well, if they haven't a bell, 'ow do they let thi know when it's last orders? Do they just shaht it aht or what?"

"No, no, no," explains Allen. "When I said 'there isn't one', I didn't mean there isn't a bell. I meant there isn't a closing-time..."

Both drivers and I halt in our tracks to consider this notion. After a considerable silence, Stan is first to speak:

"Did Ah 'ear thi reight, Allen? Dusta meean there's no closing time?"

Allen nods wisely.

"'Od on a minit," ponders a bemused Eric. He nudges Stan and winks surreptitiously before continuing his educational conversation with the Head of Lower School.

"Allen, owd lad, ar ta sure of thi facts? Dusta meean that tha can sup fer as long as tha wants an' no bugger calls 'time' on thi," he asks, his   bottom jaw almost parallel with "*le trottoir*".

Allen nods wisely.

"Well what we waitin' fo'," I hoot in Shoddy Town Speak, and I make a dash for the nearest "b*ar/tabac*". Stan 'n' Eric are hot on my heels, but Allen and Milton follow at a more leisurely man-of-the-world pace.

A few minutes later, we are all seated in a smoky corner, listening once again to Allen's words of wisdom. Leaning back in his corner seat, he folds his arms and nods knowingly towards the neat rows of coloured bottles ranged on the shelves behind our friendly barman, who we discover is called Antoine.

"Now what we need to do is start at the first bottle and have a go at *each* bottle across *each* shelf until we get to the last one," pontificates Allen. "By then, it'll just about be time to go back to the hotel. Milton, it's your responsibility, as Leader of the Trip, to buy the first round..."

Milton conducts the transaction with Antoine in his best French, while Allen lolls back expectantly in his corner seat. In the twinkling of an eye, we are all sitting in front of a glass of vividly bright yellow liquid, purchased from the very first bottle on the left hand side of the very first shelf. Peering suspiciously at my drink I am moved to ask a very important question:

"What is it, Milton?"

"I have absolutely no idea," replies our Leader, "but it smells OK. Cheers everybody!"

He lifts the glass and downs the contents in one swift gulp.

After a hearty "Cheers" all round, the rest of us all follow suit and our night out swings into gear.

Anxious to impress, I leap to my feet to buy the next round. Our first drink has lasted for all of forty-five seconds, so it's going to be a long night. I approach the bar where the smiling Antoine awaits my order.

"*Bonjour monsieur,*" I say confidently. "*Je voudrais cinq boissons de la deuxieme bouteille, s'il vous plait.*" I indicate the second bottle on the first shelf.

Antoine nods. "*Ah bon, monsieur,*" he smiles and cheerfully places five glasses on a tray. Taking the second bottle from the left on the top shelf, he carefully fills each glass with a bright blue liquid.

"*Et voilà monsieur,*" he says and passes me the tray over the bar.

I return to our table with a swagger where the others are too concerned with the contents of their glasses to have noticed my very impressive linguistic display.

"Wait woll Ah get back to t'Black Bull," smiles Stan, "an' tell 'em Ah've bin suppin' blue ale! They'll nivver believe it! They'll be fair capped - all on 'em."

He holds up his glass to the light, inspects the vivid blue liquid briefly before swiftly swallowing it in one.

A couple of hours later, following Allen's specific instructions to the letter, we have reached the middle of the second shelf and we are eying up the vivid green liquid in the ninth bottle along. Focussing our already bleary eyes across such a distance proves to be quite difficult, and we sit in a line, peering into the dim light beyond Antoine's shoulder.

The consensus of opinion throughout the group is that it is Eric's turn to buy a round.

He peers drunkenly round the table at his glassy-eyed drinking partners and opens his mouth to speak. No discernible speech issues forth, only a high-pitched "peep" which gives Eric some cause for concern. He knits his brow earnestly and has another go. There is another high-pitched "peep".

The rest of us collapse in fits of drunken laughter, but Eric is far from happy. He drags himself desperately to his feet, draws in a massive intake of breath and looks carefully at the table in front of him. He is panic-stricken.

"Ah can't talk! Ah've forgotten 'ow ter spayk! 'Elp mi, somebody! Ah've bin struck dumb!"

Stan comes to the rescue of his terrified co-driver. "Shut thi gob, yer daft bugger! Ah mek ner wonder tha's fergetten 'ow ter spayk - it's thy rahnd, that's why."

"Nay, 'as it got rahnd ter me ageean," says Eric, the panic about his inability to speak over in an instant. "Reight, what we 'avin'?"

"Shum of that green shtuff," mumbles Allen Lawton who has slumped down so far in his corner seat that only his head and shoulders are visible over the top of the table. "B'oll number nine, shecond shelf. An' make it shnappy!"

Eric rises from his seat and glides across to the bar, as if on a lightly blown zephyr of French air. He demands the attention of Antoine the Barman in his very best, albeit drunken, Shoddy Town French.

"Oh, Pierre, owd *garçon*. Ahs'll be 'avin'..." He counts in elaborate and drunken fashion on his fingers. Nodding at the second shelf, he holds up three digits on his left hand and two on his right. "That many *verres* o' yon green stuff."

"*Ah, bon,*" says Antoine our friendly barman. "*La Vervaine du Velay pour monsieur. D'accord.*"

"Aye, reight enough," replies Eric. Unable to maintain an upright stance for any longer, he staggers back to his seat and slides gracefully onto the floor next to it.

Meanwhile Antoine, carefully stepping over the prostrate Eric, delivers our order on a tray. With a flourish, he places a glass of sparkling, deep green liquid in front of each one of us.

Stan attempts to focus his already crossed eyes on the glass before him and after several attempts, gives it up as a bad job. He grabs the glass with both hands and downs the drink in his customary one-gulp fashion.

"By! It 'as a kick to it 'as yond," were his last words of the evening as his head hit the table-top and he passed into drunken oblivion.

Meanwhile, Eric has slipped into a deep slumber on the floor beside his chair and Allen Lawton, having already seen off his glass of green *Vervaine du Velay*, is greedily eyeing up the spare glass abandoned by Eric. Cross-eyed, he turns to Milton who is desperately attempting to clamber to his feet in preparation for departure.

"Milton," enquires Head of Lower School. "Milton, dear old chap. Head of Frensh Depar'men'. As Eric sheems to have gone to shleep and losht int'resh in his drink, I wonder if you might gi' me your permish'n to finish it off for him?"

"Carry on, Allen," replies Milton over his shoulder as he makes for a point in the bar-room about six feet to the left of the exit door. "You are ver' welcome."

Now, over the past thirty minutes or so, Yours Truly has also begun to feel the effects of the Allen Lawton drinking technique. I note very carefully that there are three Milton Prestons making their ways across the bar-room to the exit while I remain slumped in my chair next to a pair of Allen Lawtons. I am also amazed to see that we now have four drivers on our trip, two of whom are fast asleep on the floor.

My Inner Shoddy Town Voice informs me of my current state: "*Ah've an idea as tha'r pissed, owd lad. Ah reckon it's time as tha med fer thi bed.*"

This was indeed sound advice.

I leapt to my feet instantly to make my way back to the hotel where a nice clean pair of sheets awaited my presence. But at this vital moment, my legs decided that they belonged to somebody else and buckled under the currently unfamiliar pressure of attempting to walk. In a trice, I was on all fours crawling towards the exit through which all three Miltons had now passed onto the street outside.

I turned to wish our host, Antoine, a very French goodnight. "Bonshower, mon shewer," I giggled, and crawled drunkenly down the steps...

Out on the street, the three Miltons are long gone. I look about me in a forlorn attempt to establish my location. This proves to be quite difficult from my current position - on my knees. Sensing that I am lost in a foreign country, I turn back to the steps of the "*bar/tabac*". Both Allen Lawtons are manfully poised on the second step, their left legs waving about in front of them, attempting to descend to the third.

I hoist myself erect, wave a drunken finger at the left-hand of the Allens and proceed to address our Heads of Lower School: "Mishter Lawton, shurr, I think I am losht. Do either of you two happen to rem'er the way back to the hotel?"

"Fear not, young Butler," both Allens reply confidently. "We shall negosh'ate our way by telepathy!" Setting off at a drunken trot, each Allen waves an imperious arm towards the end of the street.

Instructing both my legs in Shoddy Town Speak: "C'mon, yer buggers! Do thi job," I set off after the Allens as they disappear round that dimly-lit French corner of 1967...

And to this very day, I have no recollection of how I ended up between the afore-mentioned sheets in my hotel bed-room. But the following morning finds me alive and well and tucking in to my coffee and croissants - a fully-fledged graduate from the Allen Lawton School of Alcohol Consumption, albeit with a very thick head...

Later that same morning, the BHS party boards our coach and we are welcomed by Stan 'n' Eric. Each sports a fixed grin and a glassy stare, and they move about the drivers' compartment as if in the direst pain. They are practising their 70 mph change-over routine in *very* slow-motion.

"Just mekkin' sure we know what we're doin," offers Stan by way of explanation, sinking slowly into the driver's seat alongside the sluggishly slow-to-move Eric.

"Tha'll 'a' ter be sharper ner that, Eric owd lad," he mutters to his co-driver. "Else Ah's'll crush thi cigs in thi jacket pocket. Nar come on - once more - as fast as tha can."

I leave them to it and make for a window seat where I can spend the four-hour journey down the "autoroute" well away from our drivers' gymnastic change-overs. I need to sleep off the effects of the Allen Lawton Tuition Session before we arrive at our accommodation in Cap d'Ail...

After a fairly uneventful journey during which several driver-changes take place at a modest seventy mph, we are approaching the south coast of *La Belle France* in teeming rain. We have travelled at break-neck speed over the last twenty or so miles in the effort to reach our destination before nightfall, but to no avail.

As the dark clouds gather ominously above us and night begins to fall, we draw to a halt by the side of a narrow mountain road to consult the map. The teachers in charge and both drivers scrutinize the cartographical information in front of them without much success.

There is a great deal of head-scratching and sucking in of cheeks, but eventually, after peering at the route-plan in the gathering gloom for a full ten minutes, Milton discovers that in order to reach our "*campe de vacances*" beside the Mediterranean Sea, we are faced with a choice of two roads. Both of them involve many twists and turns on hair-pin bends and a very steep descent, so Head of French consults the Joint Committee of Drivers, Stan 'n' Eric.

The last-named gazes doubtfully at the map. After even more head-scratching and sucking of cheeks, Eric makes a positive contribution: "What dusta think abaht it, Stan?"

"Well, Eric, Ah've counted all t'bends on booath rooads, an this un 'ere 'as t'least, so that's t'one we's'll tek. Awreyt, owd lad?"

"Reight enough, Stan," nods Eric. "Come on then, lerrus ger agate afore it's ter dark ter see. Besides, Ah'm bloody starvin'."

Having democratically agreed our route, both drivers leap to their stations aboard the bus and we proceed with the descent. It is now very, *very* dark and the rain continues to teem as the bus negotiates the narrow winding road down to the coast.

Some of the hair-pin bends are so tight that the coach has to perform three-point turn manouevres in order to get round them. An additional hazard was the proximity of the steep drop into the seemingly bottomless abyss at the side of the road.

I well recall staring out of the window beside me into an empty chasm not three feet away, as Stan 'n' Eric jointly performed a particularly tight three-point turn. Looking round, I noted several white-faced Shoddy Town lads as they contemplate the prospect of a six hundred feet tumble down the mountainous slope into the pitch black of the French night.

About an hour later, in the thick, velvet darkness of the soaking Mediterranean night, we finally arrive at our camp-site. As we alight from our coach, the echoes of Milton's January promise of "wall-to-wall sunshine every day of our stay" seemed to have all the hallmarks of A Great Big Porky. All in all, we are tired, dishevelled and hungry. Recovering from our recent death-defying coach-journey down the mountain side, we are not at all thrilled to be here on the Riviera coast.

Allen Lawton begins the rumblings of protest as he rails at the will of the Weather Gods. "Well, we've come all this way to get soaked by foreign rain. I could have stayed at home and got just as wet on Commercial Street, Milton."

Milton is apologetic, mistakenly feeling that he is responsible for the poor quality of the French weather "I am very sorry, Allen. But just wait until you see the view across the bay in the morning. It'll take your breath away."

But before he can add any further apologies, *Monsieur le Patron*, the Camp Manager, approaches at a trot and engages Our Leader in some very rapid French conversation. The outcome results in our party being led along dimly-lit alleyways between fairly spartan tin-huts, the so-called "chalets" of the camp-site. There are further rumblings of discontent from the Head of Lower School as we traipse through the soaking rain, desperately hoping that the next "chalet" is the one allocated to us.

Just as the rain has begun to run in rivulets down my back, it is left to Butterworth, a second year lad, to relieve the tension of the moment.

Bright faced, beaming and utterly oblivious to the current climatic conditions, he races along the line of Shoddy Town lads and stops immediately in front of Milton, the Trip Leader.

His face is lit by a radiant smile of pure satisfaction as he hops up and down excitedly before Milton with his hand up, classroom-style, to ask a question.

"Well, lad! What is it," asks an exasperated Milton, fast approaching the end of his Head of Department's tether.

"Sir," beams Butterworth enthusiastically. "Please, Sir, can we go swimmin'?"

My memory fails me as to Milton's precise reply, but I *can* recall the image of Butterworth scuttling along one of those dark alleyways and disappearing into his allocated chalet with his proverbial tail between his legs ...

After a short settling-in period, the whole party is conducted to the camp restaurant for a hearty supper. During the main course, feeling the hunger-pangs generated by the long journey and the lousy weather, I am sorely tempted to declare to Milton that the serving of meat placed before him looks suspiciously like "cheval".

This would have undoubtedly guaranteed me a double helping, but I take pity on our under-nourished Trip'Leader and keep my thoughts to myself. After all, it is to be my privilege to be sharing a chalet with Milton, and I don't wish to upset him before turning in for the night.

So, after our refreshingly hearty meal in the camp restaurant, all members of the BHS party returned to their quarters, still very wet but at least well-fed and watered. And not long after that, in our iron-framed bunk-beds, Milton and I were being lulled to sleep by the steady patter of rain-drops on the tin-roof of the chalet.

I vividly recall waking the following morning with the bright sunlight dazzling me into new-day consciousness. Eagerly donning my Riviera-style holiday clothing, I rush to the door of the chalet and throw it open. The vista which confronts me is amazingly breathtaking in all its splendour.

The rays of the early-morning sun wrap me in a wave of warmth as I shield my eyes and confront the vast expanse of sparkling Mediterranean blue, not eight hundred yards from the chalet doorway. Below me, a slope of lush green vegetation surges in swathes down to a ribbon of silvery sand which stretches either side as far as the eye can see. Whispering waves lap gently onto the shore - and there is not a cloud in the sky.

The entire panorama is nothing less than idyllic.

I stand, open-mouthed in wonder at the prospect of such a magnificent view. But my moment of silent, awesome contemplation is shattered by the patter of First Year feet and the excited chatter of Shoddy Town voices. Tearing my gaze away from the magnificence of the Mediterranean coast in front of me, I look along the line of chalets. Butterworth and several of his chums are racing enthusiastically towards me.

They screech to a halt immediately in front of me. Bubbling over with adolescent glee, each lad wafts his hand in the air, as if still back in our Batley classroom .

"Sir," they chorus excitedly. "Please, Sir, can we go swimmin'?"

***

THANKS FOR

THE MEMORIES

Strolling along the footpath beside Lydgate Junior School, not far from our Soothill semi-detached of a few years ago, I pause for a few idle moments and gaze across the vista that spreads out below me. The green fields above Grange Road tumble down to the railway viaduct and the back of the station yard. Beyond, modern-day Batley sprawls the length of Bradford Road and back along Commercial Street, the old Shoddy Town image long-gone, but not forgotten. A host of different businesses have taken over the mill-buildings of yester-year, bringing a far-different economic life to the town of my youth.

And as I gaze, my mind's eye wanders wistfully up Branch Road and comes to rest just past the old bus station. A blue capped file of thirteen year-old lads is waiting to cross the Market Place on their way to the Baths on Cambridge Street. It's 1958 again, the Town Hall clock is striking the hour and we Batley Grammar School lads are preparing for yet another swimming lesson with Harold Blackburn...

One of the delights of spending almost a lifetime in the Shoddy Towns is that on a daily basis, I can trace my footsteps back over the years, pass up the snickets of my youth and chase down the ginnels of time gone by. I've been allowed a trip "over yonder" to a joyful past where my fairly ordinary tales have become severely embellished for the purposes of a "reight good laugh".

But the real delight lies in the fact that I can re-live these tales of mine almost every day on my travels around the Shoddy Towns. As an old man, I have time to stand and stare as I pass by those evocative spots of memory, and wherever I pause for a few nostalgic minutes at some road-side, the mists of time roll back, and I'm fifteen once again.

Connie Francis still thinks Cupid is Stupid, Danny and the Juniors remain at the Hop and Eddie Cochrane wallows in his Summertime Blues. But all too soon, the strident notes of yesterday's rock n' roll hits float away on the clouds of my memory and it's Twilight Time with the Platters. Returning to the bright lights of the present-day isn't always easy...

My parental home on Huddersfield Road is still there, just above the whale-bone arch and the Bar House shop. But it's almost unrecognisable now with its extensions and refurbishments, and the Bar House no longer sells the "Great Little Cigarette" at five for ninepence. Dopey Don has long since ceased his scooter journeys along Bradford Road, but he is well looked after in a care home in Dewsbury. Eric the Fireman surrendered his fire-report notebook and took "early retirement" some years ago.

My Mud Bath haunts and the Docker Tree, opposite the Grammar School on Carlinghow Hill, have long since disappeared under the weight of a modern housing devel-opment, as has John Crossland's Builder's Yard up

Hightown where I learned many of my lessons for life. I often pass by and stare across at all the new semi-detached houses in their tasteful development where once we loaded up "t'wagon" with equipment for our day's toil.

Echoes of Peter Leary's "Relax! Let Capstan take the strain" come floating across Halifax Road as I look at the neatly cemented joints of the brick-work on the house-walls. From somewhere in the heavens high above me, I hear again those 1967 instructions: "Fower ter one, Freddie owd lad. Fo' t'bricklayin', it's allus fower ter one"...

A recent stroll down Croft Street in Heckmondwike towards the Palace Cinema revealed that the red-brick building of my spotty youth is still there, casting a looming shadow across the street. But there'll be no more cat-calls in the middle of the Saturday night feature now, because these days it echoes to another, more modern call of bingo. The infamous fire-exit door, however, still shouts at me. As I stand and stare, I think I can just make out on its face the remains of a faint yellowing stain...

So all in all, telling these tales of mine for the enjoyment of others has been something of a selfish exercise. I've been privileged to take people on a trip down memory lane, back to a time when our Shoddy Town lives seemed much simpler and less complicated than those of our modern-day counterparts. A game of football on a Saturday afternoon, half-a-crown's worth of double-seated darkness at the Palace or a few pints of Hammonds Bitter at the Little

Saddle - and the world was ours. The tales of such esca-
pades would reverberate endlessly around the corridors of
Batley Grammar School, enough to keep us entertained
until next week at least, when we'd do it all over again...

So now, it's time to continue on my Shoddy Town way -
"over yonder" - back to the time when Taylor's Mill still
belched thick black smoke, Dewsbury RLFC still played at
Crown Flatts and Eric the Fireman still raced along
Westgate at the first sound of the Heckmondwike fire siren.

Ever since 1958, I have become heartily grateful to *all* the
people of the Heavy Woollen District whom it has been my
privilege to encounter. *They* have given me, free of charge,
the raw material for my tales and a good few laughs on my
wanderings around Batley, Dewsbury and the Spen Valley.
So to all those genuine Shoddy Town folk who have joined
me on my 45-year journey for a "reight good laugh", my
sincere thanks. Each and every one of you has made a
happy man feel very old!

***